The Key to Gen Z

Unlocking the Digital Generation

Andrew Whitmire

© Copyright 2024 - All rights reserved.

By reading this document, the reader agrees that under no circumstances is the author responsible for any losses, direct or indirect, that are incurred as a result of the use of the information contained within this document, including, but not limited to, errors, omissions, or inaccuracies.

Table of Contents

Introduction

Have you ever wondered what *rizz, big yikes, stan,* and *cap* means, when the last time you checked, *Stan* was the name of your uncle and *yikes* was something Scooby Doo said when he saw a ghost? Do you ever feel lost and overwhelmed stepping into your teenage brother, sister, or child's room? All of a sudden, you're faced with a generational divide that feels like the Great Wall of China?

And worst of all, are you tired of the baggy jeans and bucket hats? Or are you confused as to why Gen Z is climbing into your closet every now and again to steal all your old college outfits from the nineties?

Let's admit it. Gen Z isn't easy to understand. Sometimes it feels like they are little foreigners living in the same house, speaking gibberish and sitting on their phones, scrolling for hours on end, listening to the same little dingle over and over again. Or even worse... rap music that sounds like kitchen noises. They do silly little dances and make plenty of silly jokes that all fly over our heads. For a moment, we've never been further away from something that has, at some point, been inside of our bodies fifteen or so years ago.

Gen Z is complicated.

And the complicated part is the fact that these kids call *us* extra. They call us complicated. They call us cheugy and high key, whatever that means. But let me tell you something, Mom and Dad. Gen Z isn't that complicated, and neither are you.

Gen Z is the moment you open up your phone. It's when you open up the home screen of Netflix.

But before we get into the nitty-gritty, let's take a second to look at how our world has integrated with Gen Z. You'll find Boomers on Facebook and Millennials on Instagram. There is no shame in being any one of them, but let me tell you, Gen Z is on a platform that has haunted all our parental dreams. TikTok. And TikTok isn't like any other—it's short-form videos, where now, our memes aren't just pictures anymore. The memes move in video format.

The last thing you need to do is stress, fam! *The Key to Gen Z* is here to be your sherpa through this wild journey of understanding your Gen Z child or your Gen Z friend, and better yet, cherishing that relationship with them. Now, we won't turn you into a Gen Z kid or try to change you, but we will help you understand your Gen Z child. Written by a Millennial who's just as shaken by Gen Z's lingo and antics as you are, this book is your passport to the land of clout, flexing, and squad goals.

So what's the tea with Gen Z anyway? They're the ones who speak fluent memes, who can roast you with a single emoji, and who've never known a world without Wi-Fi. They're out here living their best lives, unapologetically being their authentic selves, and we're just trying to keep up.

The Key to Gen Z isn't just about decoding the latest slang or mastering the art of the selfie. It's about getting inside the heads (and DMs) of Gen Z and understanding what makes them tick.

So grab your AirPods, ditch the skinny jeans (sorry, they're so last season), and get ready to flex on the 'Gram as we embark on this lit journey through the world of Gen Z. It's gonna be a vibe, a whole mood, and maybe even a little sus at times, but hey, that's just how we do. Let's finna' do it!

Chapter 1: Who Is Gen Z?

Every single generation has been confused as to when, what, and where Gen Z actually started. We knew that Gen Z started somewhere and that their behavior was remarkably different than that of every other generation, but where did we even start with the looking process?

But why would we even want to put up a wall between generations in the first place?

Well, by creating generations, we make it possible for scientists and ourselves to examine each generation at different stages of their lives. We can compare their schooling careers; for example, most millennials probably remember spending it in front of a computer or reality TV, whereas Boomers (more about them later) remember their childhood as one where they were running around outside in the backyard or playing baseball with their friends after school in the local park.

The main reason we separate these generations into groups is to see what the impact of change is. What do social shifts, technological advancements, and crises do to a group of people? How do they react to it? How does it change their view of the world? (Dimock, 2019)

By forcing people into generational groups, we allow ourselves to understand exactly what they think and how they would react as a whole. It's like creating a stereotype despite the fact that we tell ourselves never to stereotype. The problem is... stereotypes are there for a reason, and if they weren't there, we wouldn't be able to understand certain individuals.

Now, let's get to the two most recent generations. Millennials and Gen Z.

Who Are Millennials?

Before we just hop into the understanding of Gen Z, let's chat about their predecessor. Scientists have been studying millennials for the past decade, trying to decode yet another confusing and odd generation. Millennials are now considered the future of the world—they are the future of the workplace, the future boss, the future mom, and the future of technology. Millennials are anyone born between the years 1981 and 1996 (Dimock, 2019).

So, who are the millennials, really? They're a generation that grew up with television and computers, but they didn't have smartphones yet. Perhaps they only received their first phone when they were in their late teen years, and at most, that thing could call and send text messages.

Millennials are the kids on the block who struggle like the older generations. Most of them joined the workforce right in the middle of the Great Recession, which means they're not earning as much as they should be when it comes to salaries and wages. During their time, life became one of the most expensive activities, and things like groceries and college tuition became some of the most expensive things. You would find that most of them have copious amounts of student debt to their names to this very day (*What Are Millennials?* n.d.).

Let's have a look at the good qualities of millennials. Millennials all love technology. They grew up in an era where technology boomed—the creation of smartphones and smart TVs defined their childhood and early adulthood, and because of their age, they were so quick to adapt. All of a sudden, technology wasn't just having a computer at work to send emails on; it was at home for entertainment and to communicate. Scientists still make jokes by calling this generation Gen Me.

Millennials might be social creatures because they watched the rise of technology, but they're also socially conscious. Most Millennials believe in and fight for things like climate change because they genuinely care about the environment and the people around them. You will find Millennials to be some of the most empathetic and value-driven people (*What Are Millennials?* n.d.).

But not everything is well with this generation, despite believing it. Because of the economy and the recent unaffordability of houses, Millennials are unable to accomplish plenty of big milestones. A lot of them are pushing off buying a house and having kids purely because they cannot afford it.

Why did we go through the whole process of finding out who and what millennials are? Because Millennials and Gen Z kids are often mistaken for one another when they are vastly different.

So let's chat about why you're here. Let's chat about Gen Z.

Defining Generation Z

Gen Z is a group of kids born between 1997 and 2012. If you read different articles, they might say different dates, but that is the general time frame in which Gen Z was born. Gen Z, believe it or not, is not the newest generation of kids on the block. There's actually a generation after them called Generation Alpha. Generation Alpha is a weird generation born with smartphones in their hands.

But Gen Z—phew, what a generation! They endured a pandemic shutdown in their youth. They grew up in the middle of the development of smartphones. They're YouTube kids. The internet was accessible in every nook and cranny. The climate has never been more unstable. Economic collapse lurks around every corner. Sometimes, this generation feels like it was born into a doomed world, but lucky for them, they know nothing better, so they have been adapting.

Gen Z is defined as a generation with a digital narrative and a digital native. They have spent every moment of their lives on some kind of digital device with the internet on it. But what makes this generation so special? Well, they make up a quarter of the population in Asia (McKinsey & Company, 2023). They *are* the future.

So how do I know I am dealing with someone from Gen Z? Easy. What's in their hand? If it's a phone, then you're probably looking at someone from the Gen Z narrative. Someone whose life has been predominantly online. They shop online. They chat online. They date online. They make friends online. Everything is online. And they spend wholly six hours online, if not more, each day.

When Gen Z kids experience any type of problem, they turn to the internet for a solution. They Google everything—illness, personal issues, exciting issues. They find their news online, and before they even consider making a purchase, they spend hours and hours reading reviews to make sure that they have made the right decisions. Consider their cell phones their ecosystem. Their natural habitat. Different apps and different websites all form part of a bigger ecology, each with its own function.

But I also spend hours and hours online, so how does that make me different from them?

Well, my millennial friend, did you grow up on social media? Myspace is not an answer here. For a Gen Z kid, coming home and relaxing is not sitting down with a cup of tea in front of the TV. It is consuming masses and masses of trends and feeds curated just for them. Because they've spent so many hours online, they developed this magic of curating their social media feeds to be completely personalized, and quite small. But this doesn't stop them from inhaling social media, and it does not encourage them to broaden their world.

Alongside their amazing ability to navigate online platforms come all the downsides of consuming an unlimited amount of media. Mental illness. This generation has seen a massive spike in the decline of mental illness. Before we get into the nitty gritty of their mental states, let's explore the unique characteristics of Gen Z in a little bit more depth.

Unique Characteristics & Values

Digital Natives

I have mentioned the digital native briefly at the beginning of this chapter, but what is a digital native?

In simple language, it means someone who has been online pretty much their whole life. Someone experienced in digital storytelling. Gen Z has a remarkable talent for storytelling through zero experience, through their phones. They can make videos without being video editors, edit photographs without being photographers, and write stories without being novelists. They document pretty much every part of their lives; from the moment they drink a cup of coffee in the morning to the moment they go to bed. The moments they go out are the moments they are unhappy, angry, or happy. All of it is online.

Gen Z doesn't know a world without social media. These kids were born into social media. The younger Gen Z kids don't even know a world without a smartphone. Some of the older Gen Z kids are a bit luckier because they grew up when a Nokia 3310 phone was still cool.

A Facebook account is practically created alongside their birth certificate. Most of these kids flocked to all corners of the internet before they even gained consciousness as a child. Some of them joined Twitter when it was still a blue bird and when Instagram barely started. They've been to all the dark corners of the internet, looking at everything and chatting with everyone.

At the moment, Gen Z's kryptonite is TikTok. A platform where short-form videos are king and attention spans are for old people.

What makes Gen Z so remarkably unique is their ability to bond over the internet. They don't need to see faces anymore to make friends; their friends are right there, hidden behind a username and an anonymous picture. Surprisingly, they trust each other in this spiderwebbed network, sometimes even better than their friends in real life.

Let's give you some shock treatment. Ninety-two percent of all teens spend some time online on some kind of app every single day (Earls, 2017). What does the 8% even do?

You also won't catch these kids dead answering the phone. If you want to get a hold of them, you need to send them a text or a DM; otherwise, they are pretty much nonexistent. Gen Z is so bad at talking to each other that even if they sat across from each other in a restaurant, they would opt to text each other. Imagine how strange that must look—two kids staring at their crotches in a restaurant.

Dad jokes aside, this generation is also the generation most impacted by porn. They've seen it all. And lots of it. But it wasn't really their fault, because the stuff was right there on the tip of their fingers, accessible without permission or specific requests. A study revealed that 73% of all teenagers have seen porn before they turn 18 (Earls, 2017).

But this is not the only shocker Gen Z has dealt with. Above and beyond porn, these kids have been exposed to sexting too. To be honest, this doesn't really come as a shock since all they do all day long is text. The shocking part was the fact that 25% of middle schoolers had received a sext message in some way or another. I played baseball in middle school and wanted to watch nothing but Harry Potter, and here these kids are, sexting.

The worst part is the fact that this behavior has become normal for Gen Z kids. Usually, sexting was reserved for when a partner spent a business week away or when you felt a bit spicy, but now it is seen as a form of flirting.

Diversity & Inclusion

Gen Z is the most diverse generation yet. They embrace every part of being human. They embrace the wide spectrum of race, encouraging everyone to be their most authentic self without hesitation, regardless of their ethical or cultural background. They value inclusivity and social justice, advocating for equality and representation across all spheres of society. Diversity is not just a buzzword for Gen Z; it's a fundamental aspect of their worldview.

Gen Z is also one of the most racially diverse generations known yet. This generation is no longer a walking stereotype of races, breaking every boundary that has kept the generations before them in a box. They are diverse and multiracial, often brought up in houses of numerous races and ethnicities.

Half of all American children are of some kind of racial minority, be it full or part. And they're not planning to restrict their racial inclusivity anytime soon. A recent study shows that one in six Gen Z marriages is interracial. We've never experienced weddings quite as colorful before!

They're not just diverse when it comes to race and ethnicity, but to gender and sexuality, too. This generation is pro-gay marriage and transgender rights and wishes that everyone lives a life where they can be their most authentic. The beauty of this generation is that they refuse to be boxed in. In 2016, a study revealed that only 48% of Gen Z kids identified as heterosexual. The others all refused to box themselves in as gay or straight and preferred their sexuality to be fluid (Lange, 2023).

Gen Z also does not stand for social injustice. Or any injustice, as a matter of fact. This generation wants to make a difference. They want to put a stop to issues this world has been facing for decades, like poverty, refugees, racism, and even human trafficking. They want to change the world in any way they can. In their minds, even the smallest difference is a difference.

It is said that this generation will be the most generous generation of the future, giving money to charity and helping people in bad situations become better versions of themselves. But how can we predict that they'll be so good in the future? Well, probably because most of them are volunteers now. They are signing up to volunteer and help people, whereas the generations before them never did.

Independence Is Key

Gen X (the generation before Millennials) warned us, and their warnings scared us all silly. They said helicopter parenting was going to destroy our kids. But look at them, independent, pretending like their parents don't exist. It might be because the parents of Gen Z kiddos all took a backstep and allowed their kids to have a certain amount of freedom. This freedom has caused problems, but it has also given the generation a lot of independence.

Because Gen Z is used to doing things alone, they can do things with confidence. If they make a decision, the decision is usually thought through and confident, so you don't have to convince them otherwise. But with the negative influence of social media and the internet, this generation also has no idea what boundaries are. They don't know when enough is enough.

With that being said, this generation is probably the most naive when it comes to real-life scenarios and experiences. They don't have a lot of real-life experience, be it from consuming porn, sexts, or testimonials online; they don't know much about dating, being in friendships, dealing with personal issues, etc.

Entrepreneurial Spirit

Gen Z is tired.

They are tired of working hours at corporate, dead-end jobs, even though the older ones have barely worked them. They are tired of building someone else's empire. They are tired of the traditional mold society has forced on humans. So they decided to take matters into their own hands. They took the rules of entrepreneurship, messed with it a little, and made it their own. And not just because they had an idea that could be a cool business idea. Because they wanted to dive headfirst into being their own bosses.

Gen Z wants to make their own success on their own terms.

A 9-5? Lol. Not on Gen Z's terms. Traditionally, families used to work in relatively the same field. If your dad was an engineer, you would follow in his footsteps. In Gen Z's mind, that is not even an option.

More than 70% of all Gen Z kids have stated that the traditional careers their parents are in aren't an option for them (Sushantvohra, 2023). They just don't want to do traditional jobs anymore.

So what does that mean for the future workforce? Will we see traditional jobs in the future? We probably will, but we will see a lot more smaller businesses appear and a whole lot more entrepreneurial spirits.

Being an entrepreneur is challenging. You have to be an all-in-one solution for every aspect of your business, especially when it comes to the start-up era of owning your own business. But out of every generation, Gen Z seems to be the generation more fitted to be an entrepreneur. It helps their case that they are hungry for ownership and entrepreneurship too. Gen Z is not afraid to be a Jack-of-all-trades. They want to be involved in every aspect of their business, and they are ready to put on the hat that requires them to be that. They are willing to put in the hours to make their business a success because, in their minds, working for themselves is better than working for anyone else.

Another challenge entrepreneurs face is the consistent self-doubt looming over them. Lucky for us, Gen Z is one of the most confident generations yet and doesn't often doubt themselves. If they doubt themselves, a quick Google search will get them right where they need to be.

A good quality of being an entrepreneur is being a risk-taker. Because Gen Z lives on Google and forums like Reddit, where they get advice, they are much more educated and willing to risk it all for their business.

But not everything Gen Z does is because they're good at it. Gen Z is one of the few generations that live from paycheck to paycheck with no financial certainty. And it's not getting any better for them. This leaves them to boycott traditional decisions like marrying, settling down, and focusing on growing a financial empire.

Contrasting with Previous Generations

Other than turning everything into a meme, this generation is not really that different from any other generation that has walked this planet. What makes them different is what might alarm other generations.

Gen Z is a generation obsessed with money. More specifically, obsessed with the cost of things. As a generation, they are extremely worried about the cost of education and about the cost of living. As a matter of fact, a study reveals that 21% of Gen Z kids are worried about these kinds of finances, while only about 13% of millennials are worried about the cost of living and the cost of education (*Millennials vs Gen Z: Key Differences*, n.d.).

In comparison, Gen Z is also a generation that isn't afraid to take risks. They would much rather put more work into finding their dream job than work a dead-end job to make their dream job come true. Even when it means sleeping in their childhood house for the time being. Millennials value stability, so they would prefer working a regular nine-to-five if it meant financial stability. They are the ones who put in the hours to make their dreams come true after hours.

And the last thing about Gen Z that makes them so much different might surprise you. They are mommy and daddy's kids. They are much more under the influence of their parents than their millennial counterparts. They love their parents and will often call them when they get older. To you, Mom and Dad, that is amazing news! Your baby will be around a little bit longer than you thought they would.

Gen Z kids also take things a little bit slower than the generations before them. They're not a generation that wants to try everything. They're not pressed to have sex, which means there are fewer teen pregnancies, and they're really not that into drinking alcohol either. They enjoy the good side of life, but on their terms, even if it means a cup of tea. Don't be fooled by their slower way of life though because they're planning on taking over the world.

The generation, despite facing challenges, is obsessed with their academic achievements and what will happen in the future. They are kids who study. Kids who want to be more, just like the generations before them.

The generation is also very nostalgic, often yearning after the generations before them, like the 60s, 70s, and 80s. You'll find plenty of trends online, from *fairycore* to *grunge,* all styles that are from generations before them. Don't be surprised if your nostalgic teen scrounges through your cupboard for your old clothes!

Chapter 2: Gen Z's Interests

Every generation is defined by their interests and the past that shaped them. Think about it, every single generation faces different challenges, different cultural events, political landscapes, and social influences that form the landscape we know as each generation.

The Baby Boomers are summed up in one event: The Vietnam War. Gen X was defined by the ultimate fall of the Berlin Wall and even the untimely crash of the stock market. Don't forget the AIDS epidemic. Millennials were roughhousing it when 9/11 was still fresh in the back of everyone's minds, a hushed story that defined how the next few years panned out.

Gen Z... Well, they're different. They're built differently. These kids have gone through far more than you could even imagine. Some of them were playing alongside millennials during the fall of the Twin Towers. They were there when their parents were crushed by the 2008 recession. They were there when Barack Obama stepped into power as the first person of color in the White House. They were there during every news report of gun violence in school, if not in a school with gun violence present.

Then they were there for the horror show that was the past decade. They have seen political division, pandemics, and racial divides. The Covid-19 Pandemic. They had to sit through a lot and wait a lot, but this was it.

Gen Z is done waiting. They're making changes already, even though some of them are still in school.

Before we can get to how they will change the world, we need to figure out what makes this generation tick. What do they like? What will they change? What are their interests? And what will their futures look like in this time of uncertainty?

Technology

This one shouldn't really surprise you.

Technology is at the heart of Gen Z's identity, shaping the way they communicate, learn, and interact with the world. From smartphones to social media platforms and immersive gaming experiences, Gen Z is fluent in navigating the digital landscape. They are the first generation of digital natives. Embracing technology as a tool for creativity and connectivity, rather than mere entertainment, can encourage healthy digital habits and foster digital literacy.

Gen Z has been there through the development of all of it: flip phones, smartphones, social media, and artificial intelligence, but I don't think they have a knack for picking up old-school technology. This generation is a generation unafraid of the technology that came before. They are unafraid of using digital cameras to add an old-school grain to their social media feeds.

Despite being tech-savvy in the past and present, these kids are going to change the look and feel of technology everywhere in their lives one day.

If you think your Gen Z kid is different than anyone else... let me ask you a few questions. Do they opt for voice notes explaining tedious stories, schoolwork, or communication with their bosses? Are they responding to your long, winded reply with emojis and a lot of *pizazz*? Do they choose not to capitalize the beginning of their sentences... on *purpose*? Did they add you to a group on Messenger called *The Itty Bitty Titty Committee* with no explanation at all? Do they hiss at the sight of your light-mode phone, secretively changing it behind your back to dark mode?

Mom and Dad, sister or brother—the kid in question is definitely a Gen Z kid.

Social Media

Even though our kids spend a lot of time on their phones, they can be some of the most difficult creatures to reach when it comes to contacting them. With all these apps, no one can pick up a phone.

Social media is more than just a means of staying connected for Gen Z; it's a virtual extension of their social identity. Back in the day, when you wanted a social identity, you had to make one by going out to clubs, bars, and with friends frequently. Our Gen Z kids don't have to. They can have a social presence and a social identity right from the comfort of their bedrooms.

Platforms like Instagram, TikTok, and Snapchat offer Gen Z a platform for self-expression, creativity, and community building. And Gen Z will happily consume all of the social media platforms, or as many as they possibly can. But they won't just use it like we use it—to consume media. No, our kids have a much different way of consuming media, and that includes creating media.

When we expressed ourselves when we were younger, we used to write, play an instrument, act, or showcase our paintings on our walls. If we were lucky, we would be able to showcase our talents on a showcase night or when there was a talent show at school. Otherwise, we expressed ourselves in silence or to our friends. We kept diaries. Our kids today have a whole platform where they can share their talents. They can share how they feel. They can keep track of their progress.

If you want to learn anything about your Gen Z kid, you might as well log onto Instagram and follow them because you'll learn quite a lot about them there. You will be able to find their hobbies. Their passions. What they stand for. What they love, and even who they love.

But our kids don't only use social media as a platform for good. They use it as a platform for opinions. Finally, they can express how they feel, be it about a political topic or a product, but they will let everyone around them know how they feel. Our kids have more freedom when it comes to their opinions, delivering them freely. And the best thing is that sometimes, this opinion is respected and cherished, and our kids can find a community. Other times, they aren't quite as lucky and cause debates and arguments, but don't stress. They are fully capable of handling it. If they are unable to handle it, they will let you know.

Our kids' use of social media isn't just giving us insight into their lives; it is also changing the demand for social media.

As millennials and older generations, we are used to consuming perfect images. Magazines and reality TV have distorted our view of the world indefinitely because, thanks to these types of media, we believe humans can be perfect. We believe everyone can appear perfect, that blemishes aren't supposed to be there, and that cellulite doesn't exist. Our kids are challenging that. They don't believe everything they see on TV anymore and expect something different from the media. On social media, especially our kids' profiles and feeds, you will find images that aren't perfect. Images with their biggest insecurities were showcased. Images that are not edited.

Our kids are consuming imperfect media. They are consuming authentic media. If you scrolled through Facebook ten years ago, every model would be skinny, and everyone's makeup would sit perfectly. Today, you see all kinds of body types with all kinds of skin colors.

Gen Z appreciates authenticity. They love seeing imperfections. You would also probably find that they respond better to more authentic content online. They also love good behind-the-scenes looks. The key to Gen Z's heart through social media is through curated content that is different. Content that gives them insights. Other than behind the scenes, Gen Z loves seeing and reading up about the challenges a business faces, not to look down on the business but to appreciate the business and its content more.

Think of it as Gen Z's way of visiting the factory to see how something is made or to eat a family dinner together. The more authentic and hand-made the content is, the better the reception will be.

In the past few years, or since the rise of lockdown, we have seen a remarkable difference in the type of content created on social media. Gone are the static images, and in are the short video snippets—also known as reels. TikTok has truly changed the game of social media for Gen Z kids. In actual fact, it changed the game of social media for every single social media platform because all of a sudden other platforms had to create video content; otherwise, Gen Z kids didn't pay any attention to the platform.

This new liking Gen Z took to content changed the face of marketing indefinitely. All of a sudden, marketing agencies didn't have to spend what felt like millions on marketing anymore because traditional video ads were the most hated type of content. Authentic, short video content was in, and it was hot. Still hot. This gave a big break to plenty of small agencies, allowing their content to reach a wider Gen Z audience because of their new short attention span.

Activism

At this point, we could all just happily assume that activism and youth are one and the same. They are often spoken in the same tales that envelop the universe. You can't have one without the other. And the thing is, Gen Z is the generation with the loudest voices, and they are definitely not afraid to use it.

Activism dates as far back as humans can remember, but some of the most famous documents of activism include a protest that happened in France in May 1968. Since then, we've seen protest action about pretty much every big historical event, from the Vietnam War to the Civil Rights movement. But this activism all pushed for the same: social change. The younger generations wanted to see their government stand up for their people and, more importantly, improve the quality of life of the citizens.

Gen Z is no different than any of the generations before them in this regard. Like we said before, this generation has seen nothing, but social issues cause the collapse of the society that they all know and love, and they no longer want to stand for it. They want to see changes happen, and they want to see it now.

But what could make the Gen Z kids so anxious about everything that is around them? Well, social media. Or more specifically, the way that news reaches them just about instantaneously and consistently. Think about it: when we were younger, we had to wait until we got home before we could consume news, and some of us only consumed news for a small amount of time a day. Gen Z kids are constantly lurking on social media, and they are constantly consuming news in some way or another.

Gen Z kids don't consume news through traditional outlets anymore. Now they turn to Instagram, TikTok, and YouTube. Older generations would have consumed news through newspapers, radio, or TV. These older types of media were the kind of media you could escape. It wasn't haunting you when you went to bed—you folded the newspaper up and put it away. Gen Z kids are now taking their news outlets with them everywhere in the form of a smartphone.

With constant access to news, the age of activists is becoming younger and younger. The younger generation of Gen Z kids, those born between 2006 and 2012, are exposed to the same kind of media as adults, which means that they see how ugly the world can be quite a lot younger than some of us have seen. The grim realities they have seen have forced them to think about the world in a different way and forced them to take a stand sooner.

About 70% of Gen Z kids are in some way or another proactive in a political or social cause (Carnegie, 2022). This generation is so proactive that they are the ones who would most likely boycott any product as soon as it became socially or politically involved. This forced brands to tiptoe around their marketing strategies, and anyway, they portray themselves.

Their social stance does not protect the workplace, either. If a company doesn't share its values, four out of five Gen Z kids would not work for the company (Carnegie, 2022).

But where does the strong stance come from? Gen Z's activism is rooted in frustration. It comes from the fact that these kids are not happy with the government. They are not happy with lingering debt and democracy not giving what it has promised. It comes from the frustrating experience of being raised in the pandemic.

The London School of Economics and Political Science proved this point by conducting a study throughout the years that the pandemic struck. All teenagers and young adults between the ages of eighteen and twenty hate the government. Hate is a strong word, but they had increasingly negative emotions towards the government. You can see this in numerous pandemics, from Ebola to SARS. They don't trust the government (Carnegie, 2022).

Role models like Greta Thunberg cause major domino effects in the realms of Gen Z because now, these kids are seeing much younger kids becoming activists for the same things that they are worried about.

Impact on Behavior & Worldview

Empowerment

Despite being the most powerful generation to walk the planet, this generation struggles to decide: Am I empowered, or am I anxious? About 25% of all Gen Z kids feel empowered, a stark contrast to the number that feel anxious. (We'll get into those numbers shortly.)

All we can say is that this generation does not lack motivation or ambition. In comparison to the generation Gen Z is most compared to, the Millennials, they skip 20% more adverts, 80% of them spend more than one hour on their phones, 26% have given some part of their time to a charitable cause, and 61% of them want to be successful. That's ballsy, if you ask me (Impact 360, 2022; Lange, 2023).

But this generation can't help it. They were raised on hot pockets and episodes of Dragon's Den; they were born and bred to be entrepreneurs. To dream big. To be hardworking. To be completely idealistic. To some, these traits might be considered completely negative or destructive, but for Gen Z, it means the future.

This brings us to a thought: Are they empowered or misunderstood? Perhaps just empowered to think that there is such a thing as work-life balance and that they don't have to rush to every beck and call of their boss...or perhaps just misunderstood for being stressed out?

But Gen Z is entitled to it. They are predicted to be the most educated generation in the world, and with highly intelligent people comes a lot of entitlement (and some sense of invisibility). What we also forget about Gen Z is that the parents who raised them made more provision for them. Some of them were raised in an extremely privileged environment. This means that sometimes, these kids were fully funded all the way through school and raised with a lot more confidence, which added to their sense of invisibility.

This empowerment is not necessarily a bad thing. Gen Z feels empowered, but this means they don't need constant validation to drive them to accomplish more things. They can validate their own actions and, in turn, drive their own success and motivation. This isn't the case for everyone, though. Remember, we mentioned that just as many Gen Z kids are empowered as others are anxious? There are other Gen Z kids that require a lot more validation, seeking it on platforms like social media.

Anxiety Is the New Normal

About 26% of all Gen Z kids suffer from some form of anxiety (Impact 360, 2022). Is it our fault?

No. Gen Z is quickly becoming one of the most stressed and worried generations on the planet, due to one major occurrence in their lives: COVID-19. The pandemic might not have been the sole reason these kids chew through their nails every day, but it definitely contributed.

But here's the thing about Gen Z: They are not anxious because they are worried about their own futures or their own career trajectories. No, this generation is anxious or depressed because of the people around them. This generation is worried about the people around them—especially when it comes to the mental and physical wellbeing of the ones that they love. The most interesting part of Gen Z is the fact that they are always worried about other people's health above their own health.

Global Awareness

Gen Z is a generation more globally aware than any other generation.

If you open up a Gen Z kid's phone, you'll quickly find all sorts of news sources on each and every one of their different dashboards. Each of these sources doesn't just include news related to their own country, though. It includes news globally. Back in the day, when the news was an episode on television, or a paper dropped in your mailbox, you were limited by the type of news that reached you. This news often included loads of local news, which meant that you were locally aware.

When papers turned to social media accounts that anyone from any country could follow, it allowed the same bits of news to reach a broader audience, which explains why, all of a sudden, we get to hear small bits of news.

Platforms like Twitter, Instagram, TikTok, and Snapchat hold sway among Generation Z. These platforms not only facilitate interpersonal communication and connections but also serve as conduits for news dissemination and information sharing. They expose Generation Z to an array of viewpoints and global dialogues.

Generation Z exhibits a marked proclivity for involvement in social and political affairs, frequently leveraging digital platforms to champion causes. They actively participate in online initiatives, affix their signatures to petitions, and propagate awareness regarding diverse global issues, ranging from environmental conservation to matters of human rights.

The advent of globalization has caused heightened interconnectivity across the globe. Generation Z is more predisposed to cultivate friendships, associations, and networks spanning disparate nations and cultural milieus, thereby broadening their outlooks, and nurturing global consciousness.

Many educational institutions and entities accord precedence to the dissemination of global knowledge and awareness. Generation Z is exposed to themes such as global citizenship, ecological sustainability, and cultural heterogeneity, both within formal educational frameworks and via online reservoirs of information.

Instances of global crises and events, such as the COVID-19 pandemic, ecological catastrophes resulting from climate change, and geopolitical conflicts on an international scale, garner extensive media coverage. Generation Z bears witness to the unfolding of these occurrences in real-time, thereby enriching their comprehension of global quandaries.

Adaptability

The adeptness of Millennials and Gen Z in embracing transformations begs the question: What lies at the heart of their adaptability? Furnish these cohorts with mere tools like a laptop and Wi-Fi, and they might even thrive amidst the abyssal depths! But what enigmatic prowess propels them forward?

Across generations, there exists a mosaic of virtues, each contributing to a collective wisdom ripe for integration into our professional ethos. The synthesis of traits from diverse generations promises a trajectory of triumph in the ever-evolving landscape of work.

Without further ado, let us decipher why the synchronization of Millennials and Gen Z with change seems so seamless:

Gen Zers manifest diverse learning paradigms. A 2018 LinkedIn study uncovered that 43% of Gen Z gravitate towards autonomous learning modalities (Irvine, 2023). Eschewing the need for micromanagement, they embark on journeys of self-sufficiency, acquiring both hard and soft skills. Given their geographical flexibility, they harness online resources to hone their competencies, all within the confines of their abode.

Millennials exude unwavering self-assurance. If there were a motto for this cohort, it might well be "confidence breeds competence" or "feign it until fruition." Discontent with their current professional milieu, they harbor no reluctance to explore greener pastures. Three times more inclined than their boomer counterparts to job-hop, they confront novel challenges and skill acquisitions with aplomb. Their metric of success pivots not on hours clocked but on milestones achieved, readily forsaking hierarchical structures and rigid conventions for autonomy, purpose, and perhaps, even the occasional office canine.

Gen Zers champion the cause of work-life equilibrium. A 2019 Dynamic Signal study unveiled that 39% of Gen Z prioritize a harmonious blend of work and personal well-being. A groundswell of adherence to this ethos foretells a surge in vocal assertions against stringent working conditions or a mass exodus from organizations that curtail flexibility and autonomy. The onset of the pandemic thrust many employers into the realm of remote work. Gen Z, advocates of balance, seamlessly transitioned into this new paradigm.

Millennials exhibit an affinity for change. Eschewing resistance, they embrace novelty with zeal. Despite being pegged as indolent by some, they epitomize open-mindedness, fostering a conducive environment for innovation and adaptation. Their receptivity to change fosters organizational agility, mitigating potential friction in the face of transformation.

Gen Z: Adept with technology. A pervasive challenge among older generations lies in their inability to keep pace with technological advancements. This cohort, however, harbors no such inertia. With a quarter of them embracing new challenges with enthusiasm, they eschew comfort zones in favor of growth opportunities. Staying abreast of technological advancements, such as the ubiquitous adoption of platforms like Zoom, facilitates seamless adaptation to contemporary paradigms.

Reflecting on the mettle of these generations, one cannot help but marvel at their capacity for adaptation and triumph. What alchemy underpins their agility and success? Share your insights in the comments below.

Chapter 3: Communication Styles & Preferences

Gen Z kids hate picking up the phone. And if you tried to call them when they're out and about hanging out with their friends, you know the chances of them answering are about as big as Anakin *not* eliminating the Padawans. They're not going to pick up. But you will quickly realize that if you send them a message, they will reply to you at record speed. You will also realize that your child is a bit lazy, opting for a voice note or a voice memo, but there is a method behind their madness.

Gen Z kids have major social anxiety when it comes to talking over the phone. Or, rather, sit on the phone simultaneously with someone else on the other line. They would much rather be online, chatting at their own pace when someone else is not there and listening attentively.

And if they don't have something to say over a voice note, their emojis will tell stories. Gen Z kids love being descriptive, and emojis allow them to portray their emotions. But you'll see, these colorful little images that litter your chat with your kids are a bit... extra. When they send a laughing emoji when something is funny, the emoji is crying from laughing so much. And when they respond with their favorite catchphrase, "I'm dead," they send a literal skull emoji—a response that could not be more dead than that.

Unsurprisingly, when they think someone is foolish or silly, they will send a clown, and when someone is being sly or when they are prying for information, they will send an eye emoji. But when things go south, and their plans don't work out, expect an upside-down face.

But what's with the no-caps?

Well, they decided that it's out the door. So much so that they go the extra mile to deactivate autocapitalization in their smartphone settings. Perhaps there was a Google Meeting invite every other generation missed when Gen Z decided that capitalization and conventional English were no longer necessary. Perhaps it is just a part of their carefree aesthetics. At this point, who knows? But we know that caps are for old people.

A Gen Z kid will also add you, unsolicitedly, of course, to masses and masses of messenger groups. They spare no creativity when it comes to naming the group, but if you had to sneak into their phone, you would find a maximum exodus of group chats. Some of these groups are well-named, like History Project 2024, but other groups could be named only with the clown emoji or the melting emoji. Just know that if your group has a unique name, it's not because you're unique. It's just because it's the easiest thing to search in the search bar of whatever messenger they are using.

That's it. We've debunked your kid's technological nitty gritty, so hopefully next time they complain about your light mode screen in the middle of the day, you can easily let them know you have dark mode activated for the evenings.

In this chapter of "The Key to Gen Z," we delve into the intricacies of communication with Generation Z, exploring their preferred channels and effective strategies for fostering meaningful connections. As parents and mentors, understanding how to navigate Gen Z's communication landscape is essential for building trust, fostering engagement, and nurturing positive relationships.

Exploring Preferred Communication Channels

Social Media

We all know that, at some point, Gen Z is going to take over the world. The moment they are able to pick up the phone, we are doomed.

In the meantime, they are going to stick to what they know best: social media.

For Gen Z, social media isn't just a platform for sharing updates; it's a central hub for communication, connection, and community building. Platforms like Instagram, TikTok, and Snapchat offer Gen Z a space to express themselves creatively, engage with peers, and discover new content.

Back in the day, communication was less instantaneous unless you picked up the phone to give someone a call. You had to send an email, leave a letter, or read something in the news. Gen Z kids receive instantaneous communication. And social media is not any better. These kids can receive instantaneous news and updates from their friends, loved ones, and anyone across the globe basically instantaneously.

But this isn't the only way communication has changed for this generation when it comes to social media. Gen Z kids don't like it when you beat around the bush. They don't want to see fancy pictures with riddles they have to figure out; they want their communication and their news, and they want it now. They are literally changing the face of marketing as we speak. Gen Z is the generation of *snack media*. They will find bits of information all across their social media pages, containing punchy one-line headings and bright visuals.

We know Gen Z uses social media as a form of communication because it is instantaneous, but why do they prefer it? These kids prefer social media more than any other type of communication application because social media has grown to become extremely visible. Think about it: Everywhere you go, you share videos and pictures of your experiences. This generation prefers to communicate visually.

But not everything Gen Z does is good for them. Their consistent consumption of snack media and short videos on social media has left them with an even shorter attention span. You'd find yourself in a conversation with a squirrel if you had to sit down next to a Gen Z kid; before you knew it, they would have gone off to go find something else to do.

Messaging Apps

Gen Z kids might love their social media and consume it as much as possible, but that's not their favorite way to communicate. Yeah, they love to post their dinners on their stories and their holidays on their feeds, but there's one or two apps you would always find on their phones: messaging apps.

75% of Gen Z kids prefer to text over talk on the phone… which explains why they never pick up the phone (Hughes, 2022)!

Gen Z kids are using their phones like no one else has ever done before, like it's an extension of themselves. The apps on their phones are who they are, just the phone version of them. Doesn't it take away from the personal interaction? Well, not really. Gen Z kids have little wizard hands: they can personalize not only the apps they use to keep their attention spans and put a personal spin on things, but they can communicate in a truly unique and personal way by using these apps.

Gen Z also said that contacting them in a one-on-one message instead of bombarding them on a phone call is a much more efficient and personal way to get in touch with them. Messaging apps like WhatsApp, Facebook Messenger, and Snapchat are preferred communication channels for Gen Z, not only because they are quick and efficient but also because they allow a certain amount of privacy when featured in a chat. Gen Z is all about privacy and keeping things low-key, so if you want to effectively communicate with a Gen Z friend, pop them a text message. You'll have their attention span and their approval!

Video Platforms

We've touched base by stating Gen Z kids are visual communicators when it comes to their use of social media. Think about it. Millennials were raised on television: that was the visual content they consumed.

This could mean bad 90s sitcoms and some of the best movies this planet has seen. This includes having to wait weeks for the next episode of your favorite soap opera or series.

Gen Z, on the other hand, was basically raised on streaming services. They had any type of media available at their fingertips at any time they wanted. However, these kids moved away from standard types of video content like movies and series and moved on to short social media videos and the video content that shaped them: YouTube videos.

Gen Z consumed hours, if not days, worth of vlogs, short entertainment videos, tutorials, and music videos on YouTube. They were practically born online. They still consume media like movies and TV series, but when you look at a Gen Z friend chilling on the couch, the chances of them being on the phone are much larger than watching TV.

The other way video has influenced their way of communicating is through the way that they share their own news. On social media, you will find Gen Z kids sharing short clips of their lives, something they enjoy doing, or something that is new to them. If you're lucky, you can get a short video on the messaging app that they use to talk to you.

The other way video has influenced their way of communicating is through the way that they share their own news. On social media, you will find Gen Z kids sharing short clips of their lives, something they enjoy doing, or something that is new to them. If you're lucky, you can get a short video on the messaging app that they use to talk to you.

But Gen Z doesn't just communicate by sharing videos of their lives. They communicate by sharing videos they love. When it comes to platforms like YouTube, where the application allows you to curate playlists, they compile a list of everything they love most and make it visible to everyone. In that way, Gen Z lets everyone around them know what and who they love, be it hobbies or celebrities.

Another way Gen Z uses video to communicate is through live videos. This generation can be found in the depths of online video chats, interacting and socializing with each other. This type of video communication is a lot more personal and authentic—which Gen Z eats up, of course.

Effective Strategies for Communicating with Gen Z

Visual Storytelling

Gen Z isn't known as the TikTok generation for nothing. This generation has grown up with visuals. From watching television as kids to growing up with YouTube, Snapchat, and Instagram, they have turned into visual learners.

Don't be fooled by this generation, though; they might prefer texting over a phone call, but that doesn't mean that they will read what you're trying to say. If you are going to send a Gen Z kid a huge block of text to read, you can forget about it. Unless the kid's a bookworm, you won't find them reading more than two sentences over their dead bodies. The only time these kids probably read is when it comes to examination questions for their final tests.

Gen Z is visually oriented, preferring content that is engaging, immersive, and aesthetically appealing. Incorporating visual elements such as videos, images, infographics, and memes into our communication can enhance comprehension, retention, and engagement. Visual storytelling allows us to convey complex ideas and emotions in a concise and impactful manner, resonating with Gen Z's preference for bite-sized content.

The best way to relay huge chunks of information to Gen Z kids is through shorter videos and striking pictures. These videos and images can have text on them, but it is suggested to keep the text to a minimum for the message to be carried across most effectively.

Authenticity

Gen Z knows all the tea. They can see everything from the comfort of the blue screen sitting in front of their noses the whole day. And because they have full access, at all times, to any kind of news and any kind of information they want, they have grown extremely skeptical as a generation. They can see right through any marketing tactic and will happily scroll past you and your brand if they feel it's a bit *sus.*

That's why it's important to figure out exactly what makes this generation tick, and that's authenticity. Gen Z has a magical talent to sift through loads of marketing campaigns, identifying which ones are a load of bull and which ones are authentic, so if you communicate with Gen Z, it is much easier to just cut the crap. They can sift out any fake news, determine if a social media influencer is lying, or determine if a brand is really as good as they claim. Call them the detective generation.

With all this fake news flying around, it is also safe to say that with Gen Z's skepticism comes a truckload of trust issues, too. This generation does not trust everything they see on a screen, in an influencer's hand, or in an ad, so if you want to get them to look at a product of yours, you are going to have to put a little bit more work into getting them to trust you! But once you have gained the trust of a Gen Z kid, you have gained their trust for life.

Gen Z asks very little of brands, and to be frank, if, as a brand, you can't communicate these basics, you need to revisit the drawing board. As a brand, Gen Z expects honesty and transparency. They want to know what goes into your product. They want to know who is behind the product. They want to see your face. They want to connect with you and relate to you. And the same counts on a personal level. Gen Z wants to know how you can relate to one another, and what the connection is. They want to know that you are honest and reliable and that you're not there for ulterior motives.

My favorite example of dishonesty that breaks the trust of a Gen Z kid pretty much immediately is when an influencer is paid to promote a product they don't use. An example would be of a model boasting about beautiful skin, all because of a specific lotion for her face, when she doesn't even use it. A Gen Z kid would drop the brand then and there, because how can the brand be trusted? But if you're an influencer condoning a product that truly helped you, a Gen Z kid would support the product through and through.

So... how do you connect with a Gen Z kid authentically? Well, first off, don't lie to them. This generation is built on trust, and once you break it, there is no going back. And if you struggle to communicate with them that you want them to trust you, tell them something relatable, something true. Bonus points if it is something relatable and sensitive because they can trust you even quicker.

And be your most authentic self. Don't pretend to be someone else; don't pretend to be younger; don't pretend to be mean. This generation lives on authenticity and truth, and they would appreciate it if you were the truest version of yourself.

Then, if you're a brand trying to sell something to Gen Z, the best way to connect with Gen Z is to give them an authentic experience. Something they won't experience with any other brand. Bonus points if the experience aligns with their beliefs, like inclusivity.

Avoiding overly scripted or polished messaging and instead embracing authenticity and vulnerability can foster trust and credibility with Gen Z. Sharing personal anecdotes, acknowledging mistakes, and actively listening to their feedback demonstrates our respect for and understanding of their perspective.

Concise Messaging

Gen Z is experiencing an information overload at all times. No matter what they do or where they look, there is information galore. Think of it as the confetti you used to throw at parties in the pre-Covid era. With the excessive amounts of information and their consistent snack media, this generation does not have the attention span when it comes to listening to long and winded messages.

So how do you convey a message to a Gen Zer? Keep it concise.

Keeping messages clear, concise, and relevant ensures that we capture their attention and convey our intended message effectively. Embracing brevity while maintaining substance allows us to cut through the noise and engage Gen Z in meaningful conversations.

Chapter 4: Navigating Generational Differences

The holidays can be the worst. You have uptight moms and aunts fussing over the turkey dinner in the kitchen. Men are bunched together over a coffee table, entranced by yet another Dodgers game, and the kids... Well, they spend every waking moment glued to a screen, watching their cute little TikTok videos.

If there is one thing holidays are good at, it is bringing people of all ages and all generations together. A family is truly like no other—a group of people who all have similar experiences. A group of people who have shaped similar views and values on life, but at the same time, a group of people who can remember different events in such a vastly different way.

This is how you identify generational differences.

The difference between generations is the way that they perceive the same happenings.

The best way to identify the differences between generations is to look at art. An artist that perfectly depicts the art of generations is an artist called Normal Rockwell, an artist whose art is featured quite often in a magazine called The Saturday Evening Post. Normal painted a particularly well-known painting we all know as Freedom from Want. This painting shows four different generations, all present in one room. Think of it as a picture captured at your last family gathering.

In this painting, the family is gathered around a table for some kind of roast. The table is set in the finest china, with beautiful plates framed with the highest quality silverware. Fine crystal glasses top off the finely decorated table. Grandma, the oldest lady at the gathering, has a turkey in her hand. In the painting, she made a very questionable fashion choice, opting for a bib apron. She placed the turkey right in its place—before her husband. Her husband was the oldest and wisest man in the family, the man who got the honor of sitting at the table. As the head of the table and head of the family, it is his responsibility to carve the turkey.

The painting depicted the older generation as wiser, caring, and family-oriented. The important thing to note is the artist's rendition of the event. He saw a family with a home-cooked meal. A grandmother and a grandfather who took care of each other and their young family members.

C.F. Rockwell, another artist, took this exact painting but tipped it on its head. Instead of bringing out a freshly grilled turkey, Gran brought out a store-bought turkey. It didn't seem like anyone around the table was planning on eating, either, because instead of having a beautifully decorated table, their table was decorated with plastic packets and premade food they found in the supermarket.

This simple piece of art just shows you the power of generations.

If Gen Z had to spin this artwork on its head, they wouldn't even have food on the table. You would see cell phones with Doordash orders on the screen. As a matter of fact, there would be no one seated at the table before everyone was in front of a TV screen, staring at a smaller screen in their hand.

But that is a misconception. We have our own opinions on every single generation, much like the artists above had, but the truth is, we never know what these generations are really like. Sure, stereotypes exist for a reason, but we always beg and plead for people not to judge us. Never mind painting a painting about our generation's weaknesses.

So what makes Gen Z weak? Why do we not understand who they are? And who are they really?

Unmasking Misconceptions

Gen Z is lazy. They are entitled. They are outlandish. And damn, why are they demanding so much?

It might be good to know that these assumptions, these stereotypes, have existed for generations before them too. We were all once young and dumb, and old people love to make fun of younger people. I mean, if you think about it, just yesterday, Millennials were considered lazy, narcissistic, and developmentally a bit behind... Well, older generations believed Millennials were stupid, to put it bluntly. My favorite common misconception about the millennial generation is that they couldn't afford down payments on their homes because they were hyper-focused on buying avocado toast.

The point we are trying to make: Every generation has a stereotype from their young days. As we said, older people enjoy picking on younger people.

But is Gen Z lazy? Are they entitled? Or is this just a stereotype that arose because certain generations like picking on others? Well...let's explore!

Gen Z Is Needy

It's not the first time someone called Gen Z needy, and it probably won't be the last time that they are labeled as needy either. At first glance, this generation does appear to be more needy than others. They need constant reassurance, constant transparency, flexibility, purpose, and mobility in their careers and their home lives. To many, all these demands seem pretty tough to obtain.

But if you think about it, are these demands really as outlandish as you think they are? Or are they perfectly reasonable for a generation that knows their own-worth?

The problem is that Gen Z is going to make up 27% of the workforce in a few years. That means you won't be able to run away from these claims that they demand any time soon, especially when it comes to working. They're a generation that demands change, and they demand change where they work. Gone are the long hours and strict work schedules. Why? Because what's the point of living if you're living in an office your whole life? What's the point of living if you're not living at all?

Gen Z is also a generation that understands that a more flexible schedule is possible. With the rise of the pandemic, these kids were forced to go to school online. Before then, school was deemed one of those essential life activities you could not get away with online—you always had to sit in a class, snoozing off to a teacher's long tale about some historical event. Before the pandemic, it was hushed that school could be done in a flexible way. Unfortunately, we let Gen Z know that strict activities like school and work don't really need a strict schedule, and now they're gunning for a more flexible one.

Do these demands make them more needy? No, because they don't need you when they work from home. They are just fighting for freedom. Fighting for goals. Their demands seem needy and exceptional, but think about it: they grew up in an exceptional time. They grew up during a pandemic and with the rise of Artificial Intelligence. They grew up knowing that they were going to make a change.

Gen Z Can Solve All Our Tech Problems

We've all been there. We're struggling with a piece of technology; it's not working in our favor. So who do we turn to? The closest young person in our vicinity. A child, a friend, a colleague, or a cousin. They'll probably have an answer and a fix for you, too. They must have the ability to solve every tech-related problem; what else can explain their amazing tech-savvy skills?

Well, that's just a misconception. A misconception we are all guilty of. Gen Z is amazing with technology, but they have the interpersonal skills of a carrot. And this myth is nothing but what it says it is. A myth.

Gen Z can't solve all your tech problems. They are just really familiar with technology. The reason they appear to be able to solve all your problems when it is tech-related is because they have been working with it their whole lives. There is another quality at play here: they are curious. This generation is a curious generation, a generation with no trouble learning. If you had a textbook for everything available in life 24/7, wouldn't you also be clued up? They bring a unique perspective to problem-solving, which is why they can sometimes solve pretty much anything.

Gen Z Has One Foot Out of the Door

What we keep forgetting is that a large number of Gen Z kids are well on their way into the workforce. Even though plenty of them are still stuck in school, we forget that the older parts of Gen Z are already sitting at a desk close to you, working a job. And the most common misconception about Gen Z in the workplace is that they are already on their way out, even if they were only hired yesterday.

Bosses and managers fully believe that Gen Z workers are not loyal, and we can't exactly tell you why. What we can tell you is that this is a misconception. And a hard one at that. Gen Z will leave a position or a job, not for the sake of leaving or because they had to leave straight from the beginning. No. They will move on from a position if they feel that the position does not line up with their career aspirations. Another common reason Gen Z leaves a job a lot sooner than any other generation is because they feel that they do not have a sense of purpose at a job.

If you think about it, it makes sense. What's the point of sticking around in a job you don't like where you aren't making a difference?

But that's not the only change Gen Z is bringing to the workforce. They're taking on the workforce like a hurricane, making sure that everyone sees them from a mile away. For the first time in a long time, this generation is asking for feedback and mentorship. But the demands don't end there. Despite wanting this one-on-one mentorship and guidance in the industry, they are also asking for managers and bosses to be a bit more lenient. A bit more kind, especially when it comes to schedules and policies.

But why is this generation worth considering? Well, what makes Gen Z different from, say, a Millennial is the fact that they have a consistent hunger for education. They want to learn. They want to learn on the job. And they want to be a lot better at their jobs than when they started with it.

Tech Addiction and Social Isolation

Are you a millennial? Then you'll probably remember the slew of misconceptions and insults baby boomers threw into your court every day just because it seemed like they didn't like you. They called you lazy, they said you didn't like to work, and they said you spent far too much time in front of the TV.

But now, you find yourself in the center of the world, dictating the economy and making changes, one day at a time.

What you experienced as a youngster—well, that's what Gen Z is currently experiencing. As a matter of fact, that's the case with every generation as it starts out. Every single generation has some kind of misconception that follows them around, and that misconception ruins the generation's day-to-day life. As a matter of fact, these stereotypes follow you as you get older. I mean, how many times has someone older bullied you for your order of avocado toast and soy lattes?

Tech addiction is just another one of those stereotypes that will plague Gen Z, just like your Avo toast.

Tell me, is there a day you can spot Gen Z in their habitat without a phone? Or rather, the question is, would you be able to see a leopard in the grassland? Probably not. You'll find Gen Z for hours and hours on end with their eyes glued to their screens, consuming some form of media on the ever-changing sizes of digital devices.

But the thing is... do we even know if this misconception is true? It probably isn't, and even if it was, would we be surprised?

Today is a dangerous time to be alive. Around every nook and cranny in the outside world, darkness lurks. The last thing we need is for our kids to face a challenge in their lives that could change the course of it. So, what is the safest bet? Keep their interactions located in the digital realm. That means that most of our kids and younger friends spend endless hours on their phones, interacting with others, because they have nothing and no one else to interact with in real life, which is safer, anyway.

Although their tech addiction might have its place to keep them safe, is it a myth or a fact?

Well, that's sort of a fact: 55% of Gen Z kids spend more than five hours on their phones each day (*Generation Z and Their Phones: Separating the Myths from the Facts*, 2020). To give you an idea, you can learn how to juggle in five hours. Within those five hours a day, they spend their time crafting the perfect online persona for themselves; they share who they are, share what they love, and even better themselves for their future and for work.

With instantaneous access to the internet and pretty much any information this generation needs, you will find this generation glued to their phone screens like you will find no other generation. But with that instant gratification of finding anything you want and need at your fingertips comes a dangerous addiction.

The type of addiction that infests their regular lives. Gen Z's tech addiction has spawned something by the name of phubbing—a word that combines phone snubbing. An example of this would be when Gen Z uses a phone during Christmas dinner or in the shower—a space where a phone definitely does not belong. These kids struggle to identify when it's okay to use a phone and when it's not, which could bring lots of hurt emotions to the table once parents and family feel like the *yunguns* don't want to spend time with them.

The thing is, this is still a myth. Their excessive phone usage, despite being excessive, is not relevant to all Gen Zers. Some Gen Zers spend less than five hours a day on their phones, while 12% of them spend more than 15 hours a day on their phone. That means that every single waking moment, they are glued to the screen. The myth is true, but only to a certain degree.

The problem with Gen Z is that this true myth is causing an array of other issues and, even worse, more stereotypes. It's like a stereotype of having babies. Because of Gen Z's excessive phone usage, other older generations think that these kids are wearing glasses because of their excessive phone use. Older generations firmly believe that this generation is unable to make normal friends in normal ways and be social just because their new social circle is all a click away.

Cultivating Empathy & Open-Mindedness

Gen Z is quickly trampling over Gen Y (millennials) when it comes to numbers. Gen Z is here to take over, and scarier, yet they are here to stay.

Gen Z kids are slowly but surely taking over the world from millennials, the kids that took over from them. But they're not just taking over from millennials; they're taking over from boomers, from Gen X, and from everyone before them. Before you know it, Gen Z will be like an ant farm, infesting your whole life, no matter where you go. It's so bad that Gen Z consists of up to one-quarter of the US population.

With such a large amount of people lingering in their teen and early adult years, you realize that you need to learn who they are and how to work with them sooner rather than later. How else are you going to gossip about Karen from finance when your coworker is a Gen Z kid?

Well, you need to understand Gen Z.

Understanding the Gen Z Perspective

Gen Z is really not that difficult to understand. Sure, it's a generation covered in rizz; no cap about that, but we have no idea the meanings of it, but below the surface, they're the same as we once were. They were misunderstood.

Gen Z is a pragmatic generation, which means they value solutions more than anything else. We know they care a lot about the environment and social issues, and they seek sensible solutions to solve these issues. So how difficult can it really be to understand this generation? Well, the good news is that we already know what makes this generation tick. We know what they like, and we know the misconceptions that cloud them. With this knowledge, it should be far easier to understand them than to try to understand them from scratch.

As a generation, they have high levels of drive and motivation. They carefully and wholeheartedly care about other people, and they want to strive and work towards a diverse community. They enjoy flexibility, both in the workplace and in their personal lives, and they don't like things like schedules that are rock solid.

But the last thing we need to do is make assumptions. Not every Gen Z has the same perspective. The only way we will understand their perspective on the world is to actively listen to them. In general, active listening means listening with empathy, without a response, because as soon as you start to think about a response, you are not listening anymore.

When you listen to a Gen Zer, be it in the tearoom during a work break or around a barbeque, you need to listen actively. Listen to what they have to say, how their voices sound, and how they shape their thoughts into words. When they bring up concerns, don't argue, but validate them. By validating them, you are building trust and allowing them to speak freely.

This is a generation that builds its existence solely on trust.

Embracing Diversity and Inclusivity

Gen Z is not just embracing diversity and inclusivity because they want to be different from the generations before them. They want to embrace diversity and inclusivity because it is who they are.

We underscore the significance of embracing diversity and inclusivity in our interactions with Gen Z. By recognizing and celebrating the multiplicity of identities, cultures, and perspectives within this generation; we create a welcoming environment where individuals feel valued and accepted for who they are.

We have to remember what we have learned from Gen Z. As a generation, they are the most diverse when it comes to their cultures, ethnicities, sexual orientations, statuses, and genders. There is no stone unturned when it comes to their diversity. So when we interact with Gen Z, we need to keep all of these different aspects in mind. We need to create an environment for them where they can embrace their individuality, a space where they are allowed to be them in any shape, way, or form. If you can create an environment like this, where you embrace their diversity and include them, you are creating an environment where they feel they can belong. An environment filled with love and acceptance.

An environment for them.

And don't just sit around like a twig around them; embrace and celebrate their diversity with them. Remember, their culture is their world, and by celebrating with them, you are creating an environment that is loved and cherished together. The most important thing for Gen Z is togetherness. If you have no idea where to start when it comes to celebrating their culture with them, start off with a little bit of research. Try to see what dates are important for them, what festivals they love, and what is unique about their culture. If you can show them that you appreciate and cherish their culture, then you can gain a little bit of their trust.

This generation is a generation of learning, and the best love language you can show them is to learn about the things that they love. Even if it means you have to pick up a self-help book or watch a documentary regarding the climate crisis.

The last thing you can do is value their perspective. Gen Z, at times, is notorious for having an exceptionally strong perspective on the world, but if you take a moment or two to understand why they might have that perspective, you can understand the perspective. If you understand what hinders them, what empowers them, and what makes them tick, you are able to form bonds and have conversations with them. Heck, you might even learn a thing or two from their worldview. They love sharing information, and the act of valuing the information that they are relaying will lay a solid foundation of trust.

You might even start to play a massive role in the innovation and creativity of a Gen Z kid if you value what they are saying. This could increase their critical thinking and eventually prepare them for the inevitable workplace they will fall into.

Chapter 5: Building Trust & Authenticity

Gen Z doesn't just trust anyone. As a matter of fact, you've probably tried to gain Gen Z's trust by now, but you were met with a stone-cold demeanor who didn't want to know anything about you. But you're not the only one.

One thing you need to know about a Gen Z kid and their trust issues is that no matter what, they will probably not trust you. It doesn't matter if you're their mom or their best friend; they will fact-check you for everything. So don't be surprised when you're having a conversation with a Gen Z kid, and they pluck a phone out of their pocket to Google something quickly. That is their trust radar setting in to check if something is true or not.

Before they could barely walk, they faced global challenges like 9/11, and when they were running around a playground, the government had failed them and their parents during the 2008 recession. They saw an increase in gun violence in schools, disease, and tragedy taking lives all around them. They faced all these challenges and problems even before they were teens! Not even to think about the plenty of companies that all scammed them during their younger years to make a sale or two out of them.

As a matter of fact, only 12% of all Gen Zers trust the government, and only 14% of them trust the presidency (Kearns, 2023). But to be fair, pretty much anything is under the crossfire in their minds because they don't even trust tech companies.

But because they had faced all these great challenges and big betrayals, these kids wanted nothing more than stability and someone to trust. They value almost anything you put in front of them, and you should never overlook any of the things that they have.

If it weren't for the betrayal of these big events and big companies, Gen Z would have probably been more similar to millennials than anyone thought, but that's what separates them from millennials in the first place.

But this lack of trust isn't just a surface quality. It goes far deeper than that. This generation is desperate for a feeling of safety. They deem safety and some kind of security to be at the top of their priority list. It's not even like they only want to be safe when it comes to physical and digital safety; they want to be safe emotionally, financially, and educationally, too. They are a generation that goes to school so that, eventually, they are able to supply themselves with all these premium security features.

If there is one person Gen Z will trust, it will be an expert. These kids trust their doctors, scientists, and educators. Unfortunately, this stinks for the workplace because they don't trust their CEOs and government leaders, and who can blame them?

For Gen Z, trust is the foundation of their lives. Trust is the foundation of their communication, collaboration, and understanding. It is what their education, relationships, and sense of self are built on. If a Gen Z kid trusts you, consider that a bond you can only break with a really strong hammer.

The Role of Trust in Intergenerational Relationships

A car needs consistent check-ins, oil checks, and services to make sure it is safe to use and will get from point A to point B in one piece. Consider trusting something similar. If you want to maintain trust, especially with a Gen Z kid, you are going to have to service your trust. You are going to have to check in on it often and give it a little bit of TLC every now and again to make sure it is still up to scratch. One way you can check up on this trust—and build on it is by using communication as an oil refill.

But how are you supposed to communicate with a younger generation when there are such vast differences in the styles and ways you guys communicate?

Well, firstly, it is not your fault that your communication style is different than that of Gen Z's, so don't beat yourself up if you don't get the way they communicate. The best you can do is adapt, or wait for them to adapt to you. Since you're trying to build trust with them, the latter option is not really advisable.

Try to send them a text message whenever you feel a slight disturbance in the force. If you check in with them, you are signaling that you care, and if you check in regularly but not in an irritable fashion, you are showing them that you can be trusted. A text message, you think out loud, shaking your head. Well, don't think about a text message as an inconvenience. Think of it as one of the only ways that Gen Z knows how to communicate because that's the way they were introduced to communication when they were younger. Millennials have emails and quick messaging applications, so it is super easy for them to pick up a phone and send a quick message to a Gen Z kid. However, for the older generations, a phone call or visiting someone was the easiest and quickest way to reach them.

If this is the case, then try placing yourself in a Gen Z kid's shoes. If you prefer someone to phone you because that's the quickest form of communication that you know, then you know exactly how they feel when it comes to a text message. Take a moment out of your day to extend yourself and reach out to them to show them that you can be trusted and that you are willing to go out of your comfort zone for them. And believe me, they know you're going out of your comfort zone.

If you struggle to find common ground to communicate with Gen Z, then the best option might be to send a meme. Now... What is a meme?

If you're thinking, "Oh, but I am too old for this," then you are entirely wrong. A meme might be notorious on the internet and social media now, but it predates social media. Memes have actually been around for centuries.

Memes are a way for us to communicate differences in cultures and trends. You might have even been a part of meme culture, even without knowing it. Have you told a joke before? Did you wear an item of clothing that was forbidden by the kids? Then, chances are that you have participated in a meme before.

Back to the topic at hand: The way you can communicate with Gen Z is through memes. If you are struggling to find something to chat about, a good place to start would be a meme. And for this generation, there is nothing better than a cat meme. Adding this layer of humor will not only make you seem funny but also relatable, and this generation is all about relatability and authenticity.

We underestimate the relevance of communication between generations to building trust. Like we said, communication goes hand in hand with trust, whether you like it or not. Communication creates an atmosphere of safety and security where individuals feel empowered to express themselves authentically. In an environment characterized by trust, there is a sense of openness and transparency that encourages honest dialogue.

Whether it's sharing personal experiences, discussing sensitive topics, or exchanging diverse perspectives, trust enables individuals to communicate without the fear of judgment or criticism. This open exchange lays the groundwork for deeper connections and mutual understanding between generations, fostering empathy and respect.

Nurturing Growth

Gen Z is notoriously ambitious, especially in their mindsets and priorities. They don't learn these qualities from just anywhere, but from all over the internet (finally, something the internet is good for). Remember, these kids spent most of their lives with information right at their fingertips, so they are so used to having knowledge whenever they want it and need it. With that information, they can do what they want: Use it to encourage them and build their learning. To no one's surprise, this generation values knowledge and deems it a powerful asset to have.

The problem is that if you don't nurture these qualities, then you might just stand a chance of losing your Gen Z counterpart sooner than you think. When it comes to personal growth and learning, you need to be able to supply them with the support they need. It's just lucky that this kind of support can also build a little bit of trust.

In an environment of trust, Gen Z will be empowered to take risks, learn from mistakes, and pursue opportunities for growth. All the things that they love doing.

By building their trust, you are creating a supportive ecosystem where they feel encouraged to explore new ideas, challenge existing norms, and innovate. Lucky for you, this generation believes in mentorship: They want to learn from you. They want to see what you are doing. They want to know what you are doing. If you take a little bit of time out of your day, with their consent, to teach them a new skill, you are cherishing the trust they seek.

If you engage in an educational way with Gen Z, you are not only seeking to form a strong bond with them and build trust, but you are also investing in their futures. Remember, these kids are young. They need guidance, and they are not going to find all the answers on the internet like we think they will. Sometimes, an older generation's answers are a lot easier to understand than a quick WikiHow link to something. And sometimes, we can foster a sense of trust in them by helping them with something they have been struggling with for a long time. Think about it: when you sat around the dining room table with your dad as a kid, trying to figure out complicated mathematical problems, you formed a type of bond and trust with your dad that was pretty much unbreakable. Now imagine how Gen Z must feel if you guide them in a similar fashion through a challenge.

What Is Authenticity

Authenticity has become the new currency of the new generations. But what does that mean?

Well, in short, authenticity is one of the most important values for a Gen Z individual. At this point, it is more important than being rich and famous, more important than celebrities, and sometimes even more important than people themselves.

Authenticity is a person's ability to be the truest and most natural version of themselves. Most of us go through life wearing a mask, pretending to be someone else—someone we are clearly not. We pretend to be good at things we are not good at; we pretend to like things we don't like, all for the people we don't like anyway. We put on a face for others to see so that they won't think ill or differently of us. It's a coping mechanism for a nasty world. This type of living is called inauthentic living.

Inauthentic living is exhausting. It is fake. To a certain extent, it is quite limiting and confining because you can only wear your mask for so long.

Sometimes, if we are lucky, we can take this mask off for only a handful of people or when we are home by ourselves.

Gen Z: Well, they don't deal with that *crap*.

As a matter of fact, Gen Z questions most large businesses and companies about their authenticity, especially when it comes to specific marketing strategies. Up to 82% of Gen Z consumers doubt that a company promotes happy customers because, in the back of their minds, they are wondering if these companies are buying these customers instead of gaining them authentically (Vasey, 2023). You'll find that most Gen Z kids actually do a lot of research before they decide if they are going to use a product or not because, first, they want to define if the company is authentic. They spend hours and hours on the internet, watching review videos, reading product reviews, and researching any customer-related queries.

But what does authenticity have to do with trust? Well... everything.

If you are going to be inauthentic, you are indirectly lying. Lying breaks trust. If you are looking to strengthen your bond with your Gen Z counterpart, you need to look at your authenticity. If you come across as fake and inauthentic, then you are bound to either lose their trust or not gain it at all.

A lack of authenticity means that you don't do what you say you will do. It means that you won't mean what you say. It means that you're living in a fake cocoon that will eventually spiral out of control, and at some point, you will start to lie to yourself about who you are.

Gain Gen Zers trust by being your authentic self. Self-conscious behavior is damaging to you and your relationships, and if the people around you love you, they will accept you for all you are, flaws and all. And in return, you can trust them, and they can trust you.

How to Build Trust & Authenticity

It is difficult to build trust with someone. It is something we all struggle with as people, so the least we can do is try when it comes to building trust with someone else. Here are some surefire ways you can build trust with your Gen Z counterpart.

Be Authentic

So we know now what authenticity means. We know that if we want to gain a Gen Z kid's trust, we are going to have to be our most unapologetic, most authentic selves. But we cannot stress this enough: the more authentic you are, the more these kids are able to trust you. These kids can spot someone's mask from miles away, and once your mask is spotted, it is going to be a whole lot more difficult to gain their trust. Don't make the mistake of being inauthentic; it won't get you anymore.

And if you struggle with authenticity, be transparent. Tell them what you think. Tell them what is going on in your head. By being clear, direct, and transparent, no matter how painful it is, you are letting them know that somewhere, there is a version of you that is just as authentic as they are.

Show, Don't Tell

It is a lot easier to say something than it is to show something. When it comes to values and morals, even more so. But if you find yourself in a sticky situation with a Gen Zer, then you might want to reconsider the way you do certain things, especially things that are the easy way out.

Gen Z is a generation that is socially conscious. That means that they value their values and morals. If you tell them what your morals and values are, you are opening a can of worms to skepticism because they don't trust you yet. But if you show them your values, then Gen Zers can assume what your values are and decide if they respect them and align with them.

If you want to build trust with a Gen Zer, it is even better if you know what their values are. If you can show them that your values are similar to theirs, they can trust you because your values are the same. Values can be anything from the belief in sustainability, hard work, mental health, or the love for diversity.

But why do you have to show Gen Z you care rather than tell them? Well, anyone can make a promise like "I value diversity." But if you show them you value diversity by including diverse people in your company, in your friend circles, or in your life, then you are showing them that you are living out your values. Don't you think that makes you more trustworthy?

Master the Art of Conversations

For the first time in a long time, we are seeing a generation that wants to be actively involved in things. They invite themselves to do things; they no longer sit back and watch everything happen like we thought they would, being the digital natives who can watch pretty much any activity online.

If you want to start a relationship and build trust with Gen Z, remember one thing: communication is a two-way street. Go out of your way to include them in what you're doing, whether it is cooking or something in the office. Chances are, they really want to be a part of it. Don't be fooled by their initial uncertainty and skepticism because, at the end of the day, you are still working on that trust.

If you are trying to tap into the Gen Z generation from a marketing perspective and you want to include them in your brand, create polls, questionnaires, and votes where they can freely, and without judgment, give their opinion on your brand. Yeah, asking them might be a little bit harsh and might slap the reality into you of what they really think, but it is the best way to create a trusting environment for them.

Personalize

I sometimes feel extremely special when an email marketing campaign uses my name and creates special discounts just for me. Yeah, sure, it is just marketing, but it makes you realize that we are all truly one and the same: We love personalized things. And Gen Z is not any different. They want personalized experiences; they want to feel special. They want to feel acknowledged.

If you are struggling to build trust with a Gen Z kid, try to analyze what they are struggling with and try to create a personal help guide that is just for them. Something that only they can use to help themselves. Or if you don't have a budget, get them personalized presents. Of course, you need to know them a little bit first to know what they like, because otherwise you might make them a keyring and they might think it's cheesy.

A good idea for a personalized gift for a Gen Z kid is something like a Tote bag, a candle, or even a printed mug. A gift that makes you think of them is even more sentimental and carries greater meaning to them than just making a gift with their name on it. So, run to the store and buy a mug with their favorite FRIENDS character on it; they will love it!

Listen to Them

If you are going to ask a Gen Z person to look at and listen to your values and morals, what's the point of not looking at and listening to theirs? The key to figuring out who Gen Z is, what they like, and the type of people they trust is to listen to them.

By actively listening to a Gen Zer, you are taking in all their problems, queries, and concerns. With that in mind, you are able to form solutions with them, and in some way or another, you are able to help them. The best way you can build trust with Gen Z is to listen. They want to feel heard and understood, and they want to feel it without any judgment.

Practice active listening by giving Gen Z your full attention, acknowledging their perspectives, and asking clarifying questions to demonstrate genuine interest and understanding.

Provide Mentorship Opportunities

We have spoken about the fact that this generation wants to learn. They want to be better than the generations before them, and they are not afraid to work and learn on the job. The best way to build a bond and trust with a Gen Zer is by providing them with something they really badly want: guidance.

When you guide them through situations and help them through what they need help with, you are positioning yourself as a trustworthy person.

Offer mentorship and guidance to Gen Z by sharing your knowledge, skills, and expertise. Foster a supportive relationship built on trust, respect, and mutual learning.

Stay Trendy

This is probably the most challenging way to build the trust of a Gen Zer because you are physically going out of your comfort zone to figure out what makes them tick. But take a moment out of your day to create that TikTok account and spend just fifteen minutes there. You will quickly figure out what they like and don't like, memes, and what is... trendy.

By showing a Gen Zer that you are willing to take a step out of your comfort zone to stay on the trend's tracks, you are showing them that you are willing to change and adapt for them. You are willing to work with them. For your effort, you will not only be respected but you will also be trusted.

Chapter 6: Leveraging Technology

Gen Z are digital natives, a topic we discussed in the very first chapter of this book. However, what we have to understand is that their digital nature is changing the way we perceive and use technology. Without knowing it, the influence of Gen Z is changing the way your phone, television, and even the most basic piece of gear in your housework.

Gen Z and technology go hand in hand. And that's because, as a generation, they were born and raised alongside the growth of Gen Z. Digital cameras and televisions were old news by the time these kids were born. These kids sat in front of the television, consuming hours of strange and unusual cartoons and playing games on their parents' old phones. Sometimes, they played online games when they barely went to school. And when they finally got these cellphones and pieces of technology for themselves, they made it their whole personalities.

But this hand in hand growing up made them think about technology a little bit differently. We can see a world without it because we live in a world where it is not as relevant to us. They can't see a world without it, because it's pretty much all that they know. They can't even express themselves without it. Can't communicate without it. Can't live without it.

The great thing about Gen Z is the fact that they are pushing the boundaries of what technology can do every single day. They question everything and think about everything, and in that way, technology improves and adapts to be even better than it was the day before. They have known the internet, social media, and all these platforms and forms of technology from the get-go, so naturally, they have to question the practicality and reality, shaping our future quickly. They force us all to learn new skills, adapt to new technology, shape new social media trends, and the most important thing is that they keep us young.

Gen Z vs Gen M

We have two generations who are shaping our futures right now: Gen Z and Millennials. They are bust crafting away, determining how technology looks and works, and we have everything around us thanks to their innovation. They both grew up with technology at their fingertips, but each in their own unique way. They had to adapt, change, and overcome their own challenges with technology, yet these two generations are vastly different.

How different are they really when it comes to technology?

Well, Millennials grew up without technology. Their childhood is without anything but a television, and their memories are plagued with sunshine and mudbaths. Terrible, am I right? Sarcasm aside, our Gen Z equivalents have spent most of their childhood practically with a cell phone glued to their hands, but not as badly as we think. The older Gen Z kids were just like their Millennial big brothers and sisters: They didn't have cellphones. They had the bliss of sunshine and parks. But the biggest difference comes in their teen years and the younger Gen Z friends.

Younger Gen Z kids were all raised on social media. From the moment they were born, they had a cell phone in hand, figuring out how things work, playing games, and sharing images with their friends and family on TikTok. They have been swallowed up whole by technology and their addiction to it.

Another big difference is that millennials have to grow their social media presence. They never knew how to craft a profile or how to create content. It was a skill they had to learn. Gen Zer was born into the use of social media, content creation, and platform navigation, which can often happen in their sleep. This is why they are called digital natives.

Millennials, in some way, are still a little bit old-school. They like to find a balance between traditional environments and technology. A good example of this would be preferring to work in the office but still having the desire to have a great personal life. Another example would be having online friends and hanging out with friends in a coffee shop. Gen Zers differ greatly here: They don't mind doing remote work and spending a lot of time online, and they don't particularly care for a balanced environment where they have to go into the office. Well, half of them aren't old enough yet, but the older ones don't care. They also spend a lot more time with online friends and don't quite learn as much from physical friendships and conversations as Millennials would. They're just happy spending their time online!

Millennials do have the upper hand, though, because they are far more patient than Gen Zers are when it comes to technical issues and glitches we experience with technology. Technology is far from perfect, so we can't really expect the experience to be seamless and perfect all the time. Crap happens, and Millennials are equipped with the patience to deal with these outages and issues. A great example would be the most recent Instagram and Facebook outages worldwide. Where Gen Z kids were frustrated and angry, throwing all their toys out of the cot, their Millennial older brothers and sisters saw the perfect opportunity for a well-crafted meme and a binge session on Netflix.

Gen Z's Technology Addiction

For Gen Z, technology isn't just there to make life easy and convenient. It's not there for entertainment or anything like that. Technology, to a Gen Z kid, is life. (Dramatic, I know.) But think about it: They don't use it just for communication with friends and family from time to time. They use it to work, to learn, and to play. On a 24-hour day, they spend 16 hours with technology and the other eight hours sleeping.

So... how do they utilize technology differently than we do?

Smart Phones

This is a piece of technology we have all fallen victim to, regardless of our age. But Gen Z has a completely different way of using a smartphone, and they're leaving us all behind. They use smartphones for everything in their lives. They are using it to play games with their friends, to pay for a quick meal with a tap action (gone are the days of scrounging around a messy purse for a card or cash), and to keep themselves connected to anyone anywhere.

There is a joke. Millennials believe that certain activities need to happen on a small screen (like messaging, chatting, and games), and certain actions and activities need to happen on a big screen (like email, banking, etc.). For Gen Z, there are no big-screen or small-screen activities. Every activity is a small-screen activity for them.

Gen Z has an unfair advantage, though. Because they are so used to doing everything on a small screen, they are completely capable of multitasking. Yep, they can look at a big screen and a little screen at the same time, operating both of them effectively!

Another reason for their magical superpowers is the fact that they consume snack content. That allows them to focus on each screen in a matter of seconds.

Social Media

Every generation has been pretty consistent in the way that they change with technology. If you think about it, even Millennials have changed somewhat for technology, but at the end of the day, they can probably survive one day without it. Gen Z, on the other hand, cannot stand a single moment without technology. And that's because of one thing and one thing only: social media.

Social media has completely changed the game of technology for Gen Z. Older generations use social media as a means to brag, or to scroll for a second when they're bored. Gen Z? It defines their communication. They no longer use phone calls to chat, or messaging apps, although they still make up a large part of communication. Gen Z uses social media. They communicate with their friends, use it as a way to exchange stories and update those around them, and even let the world know if they have an idea.

Social media is no longer just a way for them to communicate, either. It's a way they can narrate their lives. It's how they find products they like. It's how they fill up their cupboards with food and products.

Personalization

With this consistent access to the internet and social media, we all pretty much sold our souls off to marketing agencies and companies to send products and advertisements our way. And, to no surprise, Gen Z isn't really upset about that. As a matter of fact, Gen Z actually prefers it when the internet uses their information to deliver experiences that are personalized to them.

Yep, you heard that right. Gen Z is okay with the fact that their information reaches businesses so that they can get personal advertisements.

This idea might seem strange and foreign at first, but the more you think about it, the more it makes sense. So imagine you are looking for a product. It could be a specific face cream for your skin type. You've tried everything, but most of it makes your skin dry. Now, if you were a Gen Z kid, you would gladly answer an online survey that would disclose your information as well as the type of skin and problems you have. So the next time you pick up your phone to Google "Skin Care," the first product that pops up on your Google search is the one that works perfectly for you. And this happens all just because you filled out a survey.

The good thing is that you spent a lot of time searching for the right product, but the bad news is... they know your middle name and the area you live in now.

Education

Gen Z's consistent use of technology has completely altered the way we view education. Traditionally, school is something you go to during the day if you are eighteen years of age or younger in an attempt to obtain a diploma that will allow you to either work or study. But the thing about school is that it was a very traditional experience. You got out of bed in the morning, brushed your teeth, and headed off to school, and for a whole day, you didn't see technology. Then you would jet off home and see technology for the first time again today.

Well, not Gen Z.

They changed the way that education is run and the way education is thought of. All of a sudden, education and learning are no longer just a class you sit in or a university degree; they are something available at all times, from the comfort and ease of a cellphone.

But this spawned a whole other problem. How effectively do the phones we use? All of a sudden, you are seeing a massive rise in things like UX design, data science, and computer programming, all subjects we need to understand how computers and cell phones work. There was a gap in the market. How do we teach a knowledge-hungry generation about the piece of technology they are holding onto in their hands? Easily accessible short courses, of course.

All of a sudden, we saw a rise in online schools like Udemy and Coursera, places that offered educational short courses for free or a penny only. The new game was learning, and Gen Z ate it up.

The Digital Dilemma: Navigating Benefits & Pitfalls

Technology is great. It supplies you with endless opportunities to connect; it built a whole generation as we know them today. But too much of a good thing can be a bad thing, too. Technology is no different when it comes to Gen Z.

The largest issue that arises from technology is the gaping hole it has left between generations—generations cannot relate to each other anymore, or more specifically, older generations can no longer relate to Gen Z. When other generations experienced their childhood, they did not have on-demand entertainment, instantaneous interactions, or knowledge at their fingertips. The rapid evolution of technology often widens the gap between generations, leading to misunderstandings and friction.

But other than the gaping hole generations face, Gen Z opened up a whole other wormhole for themselves: cyberbullying, hacking, and a whole array of negative occurrences that they often find themselves stuck in online.

We've briefly discussed how Gen Z is using technology to their advantage, but it's time to check why they're doing it. What are the benefits of their never-ending social media and technology usage? And more importantly, what are the pitfalls?

Benefits of Technology for Gen Z

Communication

With social media, instant messaging applications, and video calls readily available and yearning to be used, we are experiencing a generation who is not afraid to raise their voices. We're finding that more and more Gen Zers are actually keeping in touch with their friends and family willingly. And they absolutely love it!

Information at Their Fingertips

No one really knew if this one was a pro or a con because Gen Z has always seemed to be a bit 'know it all' when it came to information, but it is definitely a pro to have instantaneous access to information. Gen Z can easily, and quickly, for that matter, find information on anything and everything, which means that they are constantly researching topics they love and enjoy.

This instantaneous access to information is raising one of the smartest generations yet. A generation hungry to know more, a generation who wants to be better, and a generation with a shiny and glimmering career.

Entertainment

The great thing about Gen Z is that you no longer have to spend hours and hours entertaining them. Gone are the days of hosting and entertaining guests with dinner parties and extravagant events. Gen Z is pretty easy going because they can easily entertain themselves with exactly what they want. If they want to stream a new series, they can hop onto a streaming service on their phone. They can play games anytime, anywhere, without disks or consoles, and they can even find new things to do with only the click of a button.

Cons of Technology for Gen Z

We said earlier that too much of a good thing is a bad thing, and this is the case with technology. Technology might present countless pros for a generation born with technology in their hands, but at the same time, this generation has become more vulnerable and weak than any previous generation. And their kryptonite? Well, the very thing that defines them as a generation.

Social Isolation

Gen Z might be one of the most social generations that exists, but that doesn't mean that they are socializing in all the right ways. With technology right there at all times to make contact with friends and family, they don't even have to leave the comfort of their beds to chat with someone. That leaves Gen Z more at risk of social isolation than any other generation.

As a generation, they no longer make face-to-face contact with anyone, and if they do, it is over a video call. By avoiding face-to-face contact to such a great extent, this generation is risking their mental health and well-being all for a cheap thrill on a cell phone.

Cyberbullies

Where there are kids, there are bullies. Gen Z is still young, and some of them are still kids, but in the same breath, they are a generation surrounded by adult activities. Social media and similar platforms were never meant for kids, and what happens when you put kids in a place where they shouldn't be? You make them vulnerable.

The internet is not helping at all. With the option of becoming completely anonymous, bullies are finding it easier and easier to prey on Gen Z. Kids are being bullied by online bullies, but they have no idea who they are or where they came from. The other problem is that because the bullies can be anonymous, they can be even more harsh and ruthless than they were before because there will be no consequences.

You can imagine that the effects of cyberbullying can be absolutely devastating.

Addiction

This one shouldn't be a surprise since we did chat about Gen Z's technology addiction. This time, we are looking at it from the perspective of being a con.

Technology is a bad thing because we have access to everything instantaneously. This lends itself to something called instant gratification. Instant gratification means that we get things we want instantly. A great example would be an instant message. If you need a piece of information from someone far away, it no longer takes weeks for the message to reach them or hours for them to pick up your voice message. It takes one second or less, and then you can expect a reply from them.

Instant gratification is highly addictive. It is something our bodies crave because it is like receiving instant affirmation. With that being said, instant gratification can lead to a loss of self-control and can quickly turn into an unhealthy addiction to technology. It's like you cannot go a day without technology, and if you spend a moment without it, you become groggy and hateful.

Gen Z suffers from technology addiction, and things are not looking good for them.

Less Physical Activity

One of the most apparent differences in Gen Z compared to other generations is their complete lack of physical activity. Think about it: This generation receives everything they need from a touchscreen, where they can sit and have access to everything. They no longer need to move to go somewhere. If they need groceries, they can have them delivered. They are no longer required to get up and out of bed to walk up and down the aisles of a shopping center.

Paired with their addiction to technology, they spend hours and hours behind screens. You can only imagine how bad it can be to sit for hours on end in one place. The implications for your health are dire, and Gen Z is reaping the fruits of their decisions. This generation is extra vulnerable to obesity and cardiovascular disease, all life-shortening diseases caused by none other than a lack of exercise.

How We Can Help Gen Z

There is no point in shouting and punishing Gen Z for their addiction to technology because, at the end of the day, they are utilizing one of their best skills to improve the future. Gen Z receives devices to use as early as their birth, and others receive a cellphone when they are five. If you think about it logically, how is a five-year-old supposed to have any impulse control when they do something they like? The problem is that they don't. The moral of the story is that we can't really blame Gen Z for their technology addiction because they had exposure to technology before their impulse control was developed. Now, they are all stuck without impulse control and a bad technology addiction.

This new addiction has become so common that recently, scientists even gave it a name: iDisorder. iDisorder is when individuals have no control over their internet and technology usage and compulsively use technology and the internet (Hofstra Marketing and Communications, 2021).

The best thing we can do for the generation is to help them with the problems they face, like bullying, addiction, and sedentary lifestyles.

Chapter 7: Embracing Diversity & Inclusion

Gen Z is the next wave of talent. They are the future workforce, and they are definitely a force to be reckoned with. However, this force of nature does not stand still for anyone, especially when it comes to diversity and inclusion. They want everyone to be included, and they want no one to be left behind.

But why are diversity and inclusion so important to Gen Z? Was it this important to any generation before them?

Diversity and inclusion are imperative to Gen Z because they are the face of diversity. Out of every generation that has walked on this planet before them, they are the most diverse in race and ethnicity. Only 52% of American Gen Zers are non-Hispanic white, 14% of them are black, 6% are Asian, and 5% consist of more than one race (Parker & Igielnik, 2020).

But Gen Z has different ideas on diversity than the generations before them, and that's where the biggest difference comes in. For Gen Z, diversity is no longer a suggestion; it is the only option. And as we know, it's the only option because they are the most diverse of all the generations. But diversity is more than just skin color for Gen Z. It's about ideas and viewpoints.

Think about it: Everyone is different. Everyone thinks in a unique way based on the way they were raised, shaped, and formed. Therefore, it makes sense that different cultures and different ethnicities have different ways of thinking. The more diversity you have in a team or a group of people, the more diversity you have in ideas. That's what Gen Z digs—cognitive diversity.

We have to thank the internet for Gen Z's special view of diversity. We know that they are extremely connected, more connected than any other generation before them, especially with the internet, social media, and all that lovely stuff just a click of a finger away from their eyes. But what we don't see, is the fact that this easy access to the internet contributed to their never-ending fight for diversity and equality. These kids are, now more than ever, exposed to everything that has to do with diversity. They are learning about cultures, ethnicities, and identities from a young age, which means that by now, they are pretty clued up when it comes to who and what is classified as diverse. And they love and accept it all.

And through social media, seeing other ethnicities and diversities made them realize that there was no reason for them to ever live in the shadows. They want to embrace their own diversity. They want to embrace their rich heritage and their ethnicities, and more importantly, they want to share it with the world.

Another reason diversity and inclusion might be synonymous with Gen Z is the fact that these kids are fighting an unfair, never-ending battle for social justice. They want to see equality. They want to see equity. And they no longer stand for any discrimination based on prejudice. Perhaps this is because, as a diverse generation themselves, they are also under attack and also want to fight for equality.

What Is Diversity?

If you had to pick up a dictionary today, you would find that diversity is defined as the practice of including or involving people from a range of different social and ethnic backgrounds and of different genders (Servaes et al., 2022). So why is diversity such a big thing now if different ethnicities and races have existed since the beginning of time? Well, as a society, we have never been more connected with one another than we are now. If you feel like it and have the funds for it, you can hop on a plane and jet off to a new country.

A country where you will introduce your new ethnicity and your new culture. In a culture where we aren't plagued with pandemics and restrictions, we work in new and foreign groups, we move overseas, and we introduce each other to our different cultures. That's how we celebrate and learn each other's best qualities—the qualities that make us different.

Diversity is not just about ethnicities and cultures. It's age diversity. Physical and mental diversity. Intellectual diversity. Gender diversity. Diversity is what makes us unique and different from anyone else in the world. You are unique because there is no one your age or your ethnicity but you. At the end of the day, diversity includes people from all walks of life, and diversity and inclusion aim to give everyone an equal opportunity, no matter their background.

Through the eyes of a Gen Z person, diversity is how we can make the world a stronger place. It's the way forward; it's the future.

But why?

Well, from Gen Z's perspective, if you have a diverse workforce in your company, friend group, or wherever, you are more equipped to take on challenges head-on. Remember what we said about the fact that people from all walks of life think differently because they experienced culture differently and their home lives were different? Well, that's where it comes into play. When you put people together to solve a problem, and they think diversely, it means that they can solve the problem more effectively and, if they are lucky, quickly too.

This brings us to equity, equality, and the words that walk hand in hand with diversity. What is equity? Before we can understand what equity is, let's have a chat about equality. So equality means that people are treated the same way, regardless of their diversity. Equality does not take into consideration if you are a man, woman, non-binary, have a disability, or anything like that. You will be treated the same way your peers are.

It sounds like it could become an unfair gamble. That's where equity steps in. Equity means that before anyone is treated, their situation is taken into account. That means you are treated in a fair manner, no matter what your inflictions or differences are. In today's age, it could be the way policies are made out to be.

Let's think of a quick example. You're back in school. Punk music is still big, and brightly colored jeans are the fashion statement of the year, assuming you are a raging Millennial. You have a kid in your class who is in a wheelchair. Equality would mean that this kid would have to travel between classes when the bell rings and all the kids rush into the hallway. He could potentially be trampled. Equity is allowing him to leave a few moments before the bell rings so he can get to his next class a little bit sooner. He wouldn't be trampled.

This brings us to the last topic of discussion, which is inclusion. With the knowledge of what diversity, equity, and equality are, inclusion is the part that makes it all worth it. It is the way companies and people work together, through equality and equity, to work together and make a meaningful difference together. It's the part of life where you have a diverse team at work, and everyone contributes to the grand scheme of things.

But we cannot achieve inclusiveness if we don't have an inclusive culture. It's like having peanut butter without the jelly—it works, but it's not the cherry on top of the cake.

If we don't include people, we are contributing to a much larger problem in life. A lack of inclusion not only allows people to feel excluded and out of place but also allows people to face something called microaggressions. Microaggressions are situations where employees and friends feel like they can't talk to anyone because no one understands or relates to them. A microaggression is also when someone has to consistently correct someone else when they assume. Today, the most popular example of an activity that causes microaggressions is assuming someone's pronouns.

Why Is Diversity Important?

We have briefly mentioned why diversity is a good thing, but let's explore how and why a diverse society and a diverse team matter. What are the benefits of having a diverse society?

Better Problem Solving

This is something we have discussed before, but it is so important in a society today where we are plagued with consistent problems and issues. A diverse society and a diverse team mean that more people from different backgrounds and different ways of thinking can come together to solve a problem.

People from different backgrounds, different ethnicities, and different spaces in life not only have different ways of thinking, but they also have different skills and perspectives. Sometimes, all you need to solve a problem is a different perspective.

With a diverse group of people, you also get more innovation. More creativity. More strategy. The beauty of having a diverse group of people work together is the fact that they can bounce ideas off of each other, which means bad ideas get thrown down the drain as quickly as they come to life, and good ideas are developed and stand the test of time.

Better Decisions

People from different backgrounds have different experiences when it comes to life. They all experience life in a different way, which lends them their own unique perspective on life. This unique perspective allows for different decisions.

An easy way to understand this concept is to have chocolate for breakfast. A child or a teenager would think that this is the best idea on the planet, but as an older adult, this idea is remarkably silly and could cause an array of problems throughout the day. Diversity in cultures, age, ethnicity, and gender brings different ideas forward, as we spoke about in the previous heading, and therefore better, smarter decisions can be made.

Another thing is that if you put a group of people together and they come from different backgrounds, they are going to be more socially aware. If you hire younger generations in a business, like a Gen Z counterpart, then you'll see more and more of this social group, which in turn leads to better decision-making.

Productivity Equals Profits

Money makes the world go around. And the problem with that is that money doesn't always keep the employee. Indeed, a job-hunting platform was curious about this statistic—does diversity actually influence the happiness of an employee?

It turns out that 55% of employees think that diversity and inclusion are imperative when it comes to any business (Gen Z Demands Diversity and Inclusion in the Workplace, n.d.). So what does diversity have to do with productivity in the workplace? Heck, what does Gen Z have to do with any of this?

Well, Gen Z is entering the workforce, slowly but surely. The older Gen Zers have already entered the workforce, taking businesses by storm, and they have a lot to say. One of the things is that a diverse workforce is a happy workforce. And 55% of employees who believe diversity is important in the workplace are happier at the office. A happier employee is an employee with higher productivity.

If employees are happy with their employers, then it reflects in the profitability of the company. Not only will employees work harder when they are happier, but outsiders will take notice of the fact that the business values diversity. You will find more and more Gen Zers interested in supporting the business because you are protecting and fighting for a cause that is important to them.

How to Create an Inclusive Environment

There is nothing quite as important to Gen Z as inclusivity and diversity. They are a diverse generation, and we know that. If we want to connect with them on a deeper level, the best thing we can do is show them that we also value inclusivity. But how, as a manager, boss, employee, or friend, do you show a Gen Zer that you also value inclusivity and diversity just as much as they do?

Well, show, don't tell.

Identify Bias

The first thing you can do to show Gen Zer that you foster an inclusive environment is to identify bias. We are all humans. We all make mistakes. And with that, it is fair to note that we all have preferences too. So, sometimes, we are biased, and we make biased judgments based on the experiences we have.

The best thing we can do in a Gen Zer's company is to highlight any bias that we view. This could be within ourselves, within a company we both work for or even as their boss. If you show them that you know what diversity is by identifying bias, they can trust you. Remember our chapter about trust? Well, here is where it comes in again. In order for us to build trust with a Gen Zer, we need to align with their values.

If you are working in a company with a Gen Z counterpart and you can see visual bias and any unfair treatment, tell your boss. Don't be afraid to vocalize what you see—it is your responsibility as a good citizen to help others.

Once you've tried to help correct others and their bias, think inward. Think about the way you view others—who do you view biasedly? Who do you favor over others? Why'd you favor them? How can you treat everyone fairly?

Once you can reflect on what's going on in your heart, you can clear your head and try to fix your thoughts.

Value Everyone Equally

This is a difficult discussion to have, especially since we spoke earlier about how equity and equality differ. Sometimes, a situation requires equity, but only when you have more information about the situation. If you are walking into a situation blindly where you don't know the person you are dealing with, it is best to treat them as equals.

By showing a Gen Zer that you value them as equal, especially since they are going to be much younger than you are, you are showing them a level of respect. A level of respect they are going to return. You are also showcasing trust, which they can showcase back to you.

A trusting, equal relationship is one that is productive. A relationship that is connected.

Suppose you are reading this book because you want to employ more Gen Z individuals, or you are experiencing more and more of them in the workplace. In that case, you can also try to foster equality in them by running a competition where hard work gets rewarded. In rewarding situations like that, everyone in the competition is treated equally, and they are all given an equal chance to win.

Chapter 8: Mentoring & Guidance

Gen Z is notoriously one of the laziest generations we have come to know... or are they? Do we really know what Gen Z's work ethic is like? Or are we just so used to seeing them rotting in bed on social media platforms and calling it a good ol' day of *self-care*?

This generation is not as lazy as we think they are. Yes, they focus on self-care a lot more than previous generations, and they take their mental health very seriously, but that doesn't mean that they're not willing and motivated to work. Actually, this generation, or the little that has stepped into the workforce so far, has shown to be quite the worker bees. 83% of future Gen Z workers believe that some form of mentorship is essential when it comes to developing a professional stance (Khan, 2023).

But what is mentoring, and why is Gen Z so desperate to have it?

Traditionally, mentoring is seen as a relationship that develops between two people. Mentoring and mentors have separate goals in mind that they can work on simultaneously or separately, and that is personal and professional development. In a mentoring situation, the mentor is usually the person with more experience, both professionally and in life. What a mentor does is pass on the knowledge they have acquired over the years. This can range from advice to knowledge and even personal experiences a person could share. The point is that a mentor shares everything and anything to help the mentee—the person with less experience.

If you think about it, a mentoring program or partnership is an amazing way to break down barriers between generations—and believe me when I say that Gen Z has no interest in keeping barriers up between generations. They are all for thinking outside the box and living outside the box because, for their whole lives, they have been placed inside a box they never asked for.

Why Is Mentorship Important?

Mentorship might seem like the silliest way to grow as a person, especially since there are plenty of colleges and universities that can advance a Gen Zer's talents and interests. The problem with these institutions is that none of them are personalized. None of them are unique. They treat every student like a piece of cattle—someone who comes in as an identification number and someone who leaves as an identification number. Mentorships are personalized. You aren't a number; you have a name.

Mentorship is important because it is personalized. You can personalize your education for the mentee if you are a mentor. One-on-one education and help can boost their confidence and make them a force to be reckoned with in the workplace. Plenty of universities offer courses in leadership and confidence, but none of these paid courses are as valuable as mentorship because they don't have any real-life experience.

Mentorship is based on real experience where valuable education and information are passed on to the mentee—information that will help them a lot more than any college class could. This information that has been passed on can help develop strong leadership skills, especially if it comes to a lead-by-example type of relationship from the mentor's side.

Gen Z is hungry for knowledge and education. They want real-life experience. They want to solve real-life problems. Supplying them with mentorship will equip them for exactly that.

But why do Gen Z kids prefer mentorships alongside traditional education? Well, because mentorships supply them with guidance and support. They live in uncertainty, like all of us did when we were younger, and they are looking to navigate an ever-changing world, just like we are. By providing them with the guidance they need, they can navigate the ever-changing world effectively. It's like teaching a kid how to swim in a pool before they swim in the ocean. The ocean, like life, can be unpredictable and scary, and once you know you can swim, a scary challenge can seem a lot easier. This is exactly what mentoring is to a Gen Z kid. Teaching them how to swim in the ocean of life.

What you have to remember is that, as a mentor, you have already navigated through the struggles of life. At this point, you might even be a professional at it—a Gen Z kid, not so much. They need to learn how to make informed decisions, and they need to learn why they are making these decisions. And with guidance from a mentor, they can make decisions that will benefit them, not bring them down.

Mentorship also helps to develop skills that are essential for someone's personal and professional life. Some people fresh out of school don't always know how to deal with daily situations, like email etiquette, how to communicate effectively, and how often they need to communicate. Hell, even some technical skills aren't taught in schools anymore.

We always joke about saying that kids these days don't know any housework, and that's not because they don't want to learn. It is because no one is teaching them. Back in the day, we had classes that showed you how to cook and do woodwork, and today, these classes don't really exist anymore. That leaves a whole generation unable to wield a spoon or a drill.

The point is that a mentorship supplies Gen Z kids with these essential skills that they will need for the rest of their lives. They're not looking for just anyone to teach them these skills, either. They are looking for someone who can give them constructive feedback, someone who can help them grow. They want someone who can call them out on their crap, even if it means they have to take a punch or two to realize the cold truth.

As a mentor, you have people around you. You have a network. You know how to network and build relationships. A Gen Z kid has no idea what they are doing, and they have no idea how to network. One of the skills these kids are never taught in school is how to network. This means they have no way to navigate and find new opportunities, develop businesses, or even further their career paths—how are you supposed to grow if you have no idea how to grow in the first place?

A mentor supplies them with knowledge on how to network. With this knowledge, they can then further themselves, develop themselves, and build their own future without anyone's help. Everyone needs a push to start at the beginning!

One of the last reasons mentorship is exceptionally important to Gen Z is for personal reasons. Gen Z values and appreciates mentorship because it helps them build confidence and helps them grow on a personal level. Confidence is difficult, especially if you are stuck in a digital world and have no idea how to interact with people in real life.

We forget that they live most of their lives online, and the challenge with this is that they might be a bit shy when it comes to interaction in person. By interacting with a mentor who believes in them—a mentor who trusts them and sees the value in them—they are building confidence.

Without even knowing it, the mentor is improving something so small that can make such a large difference in the mental health of a Gen Zer. Confidence and self-esteem go hand in hand, and both of them are interconnected with mental health. If Gen Zers feel like they are improving, that they are doing well, and that they are worthy, their self-esteem increases, and their mental health looks better.

The best thing about mentorship, for both parties, is that you are improving their outlook on life. If you don't know many things and your views are limited to what you know, then life can look dark and hopeless. If you know how to tackle problems and how to face challenges, then all of a sudden, you have a game plan, and life looks a lot different. Life looks better.

How Do I Overcome Generational Boundaries?

You have spent a lot of time teaching yourself the quirks and mission of Gen Zers. We have gone through the motions of what they like and dislike, what their talents are, and what makes them tick. But yet, you find yourself more out of touch with the next generation than ever before. How are you supposed to mentor someone you cannot relate to at all?

Well, to begin with, you will have to remind yourself that a generational boundary is just that: a boundary. Yes, you have to overcome this boundary in order to become a mentor because if you can't relate to the mentee, then your lessons in life might just fly over their heads, but you can't let it hold you back. There are plenty of strategies you can use to overcome this blockade in your head—strategies that will help you become the best mentor yet. So, let's explore some of these strategies.

Understand Their Culture

We know that diversity and inclusion are extremely important to Gen Z. We have explored ways in which we can show them that we value their views on diversity and inclusion, and here you finally get to showcase what you learned.

The least you can do is start to learn about the things that are important to them. What is their culture? What beliefs do they value? What experiences do they have? All these things you can figure out over a cup of coffee. The more comfortable you make it for them, the more information you will get out of them. Make sure that if you are going to make an effort to learn who they are and what they believe in from the perspective of diversity and inclusion, you might as well make it casual and authentic. Remember authenticity? The more authentic you are, the more they will trust you. The more they trust you, the more they will tell you.

Listen Actively

As a mentor, one of the main jobs you will have is to listen. Before the mentoring even starts, make sure that you listen actively and carefully to all the aches and pains of Gen Zer, no matter how relatable these pains are. The more you listen, the more you will understand them and who they are. The more you understand them, the better you are equipped to help them.

By listening actively, you are also supplying Gen Zer with a kind and caring environment where they can feel supported and safe. If you want to be a mentor, this is the ideal environment to have. When they can express themselves without judgment and with support, then they can tell you what hurts them, and you can easily and effectively share knowledge that will help them.

Find Something You Share

Hobbies transcend ages, genders, and generations. If you want a stronger bond with your mentee, and you feel like the generational gap might be keeping them from sharing how they feel, try a more casual approach to things. Try to figure out what their hobbies are. Perhaps you both play an instrument, or you both love a specific series on Netflix—this will allow you to connect with your Gen Z mentee.

Most relationships are built on some sort of friendship, and what better to build a friendship than a mutual interest in Chandler Bing's bad jokes on FRIENDS?

Embrace Technology

This one might be tricky because your life might not be quite as integrated with technology as your Gen Z mentee's life would be. But by now, in this day and age, you're probably extremely familiar with technology, and you find yourself sharing cat pictures on social media more than you should.

The best you can do is embrace the things that they like, and that is technology. Bond with your Gen Z counterpart by sharing memes over social media or sending them inspirational things over instant messaging. They will appreciate the effort coming from your side, even if it is the cheesiest message to receive on a Monday morning.

How Do I Mentor the Next Generation?

Mentoring someone can seem like a daunting task, especially if you have never done it before. Perhaps you see mentoring as a second-nature thing because you love teaching, or perhaps mentoring is scary because you have no idea where to start.

The only way to approach mentoring is with compassion and patience. If you enter a mentoring relationship any other way, then you risk not only hurting the mentee but wasting your time, too. In today's world, post-COVID-19 pandemic, the world has offered a more flexible schedule for pretty much everyone because we realized that the world can be a scary place and that we need to be there for one another.

So, here are our top four tips when it comes to mentoring the new generation.

1. Mentoring Is a Two-Way Street

Just as much as Gen Zer wants to learn from you, you have to remember that they might know something that you don't know. Never view a mentoring relationship as a relationship where you are sharing information. If they share information, listen and make sure that you absorb it. You might just learn something valuable from them that might help you in your life.

2. They Need to Reach Out

Sometimes, giving advice might fall on deaf ears. You can't mentor someone who doesn't want to be mentored, so remember to make sure that your mentee reaches out. Make sure that they ask questions, and if they don't, encourage them to. Let them know that this space, the mentoring space, is a safe space and that they can ask anything they want. They need to realize that there is no such thing as a dumb question.

3. Don't Be Their Only Mentor

The biggest mistake we can make as mentors is limiting our mentees to only our knowledge. Our knowledge might be limited, and it might cause them to have limited insight, so encourage your mentee to look for other types of mentorships. You need to let them understand that the best decision they can make for themselves is to get advice and knowledge from multiple sources. The more knowledge they get from more sources, the better they will be equipped to take on challenges in the future.

4. It's All in the Chemistry

Don't force a relationship with your mentee. If it doesn't work, it doesn't work. What you have to realize is that a relationship that has no chemistry is a relationship that will not work, no matter how much you try to force it to work. The best thing you can do if you feel like you and your mentee are alone is to let them go.

Perhaps you can offer some assistance by helping your mentee search for their next mentor, but at the end of the day, it is entirely up to them who they pick. And you can't be hard on yourself if it doesn't work, because it's not your fault.

Chapter 9: Navigating Conflict & Differences

We generally don't think much of age other than the fact that we acquire wrinkles as we trudge along our journey in life, but our age signifies much more than just the type of supplements we use to aid our bodies. Our ages define the generations we are in and the generational gap we find ourselves in. Our age determines the way we think about things and our attitude towards each other, and it even dictates our behavior.

But it's not just how we age and experience things in our lives that forms who we are. There are two reasons each and every person acts the way they do, and that's where they are in the cycle of their life at the moment and the people around them. If you ever wonder where you are in your life cycle, ask yourself this simple question: Am I a young adult, middle-aged, a parent, or am I retired? You'll quickly find that many of the individuals around you are the same age, too. Sisters, brothers, cousins, friends—all the people you used to be close to are roughly the same age.

To no one's surprise, a younger person and an older person will have differences in perspectives and opinions, and that's no one's fault. The fault lies in the fact that they experienced different styles of upbringing, different socioeconomic changes, and different situations in life.

We know there are different generations and that they differ greatly, but what is the makeup of a generation? Usually, a generation is described as a group of individuals who are all born between a fifteen- and twenty-year interval. Examples include Millennials, Boomers, Gen X, Gen Z, and the Silent Generation. Some of these generations we've already discussed, such as the Millennial group. Let's chat about the different generations.

The Different Generations

The Silent Generation

The first time we saw someone mention something called the Silent Generation was in 1951 in a Times Magazine Article (Smith, 2020). Can you guess what is remarkable about this generation? Yup, you probably guessed right, and it was the fact that they were silent. They weren't silent because they wanted to be silent; they were silent because they had to be. This generation was born during arduous times between 1928 and 1946—the years of the Great Depression. But as a generation, they weren't defined by the Great Depression alone—they were defined by the Dust Bowl, economic uncertainty, war, and political uncertainty.

Can we blame them for becoming one of the most careful and conscientious generations? No, not after growing up in the times that they grew up in. The silent generation has plenty of wonderful qualities, though—qualities you won't always find in any other generation. As a generation, the Silent Generation is thrifty. Because they grew up during difficult times, they had to make the best of the situation they had for food and for clothes. This made them exceptionally resourceful as a generation. As a generation, they are also respectful, loyal, and extremely determined—all extremely beautiful qualities that make them uniquely Silent.

Baby Boomers

We've all heard the Gen Z slang term OK Boomer. And for Boomers, this phrase might bring a type of anger forward that pulsates through their veins—but Gen Z and other generations pick on this specific generation for the reason. They're not only known as the Boomers; they are also known as one of the gloomiest generations yet. Boomers are the people born between 1946 and 1964.

So, why is this generation so gloomy? Well, that's because they're answering all the important life questions with a glass-half-empty attitude. Pew Research asked a few Boomers if they felt their salaries would cover their expenses in the next year, and 55% of Boomers said they didn't believe so (Pew Research Center, 2008). 19% of Boomers even went as far as to say that their lives are far worse than the lives of their parents when their parents were the same age. If that wasn't enough negativity, Boomers also have a far lower perception of their quality of life, but all based on the fact that their income isn't enough to sustain the lifestyle that they want.

But this perception might just be caused by the fact that they are getting older. Boomers were never really quite as negative as they are now. They became increasingly negative, only because they became increasingly anxious regarding their personal finances.

Baby Boomers might have had a remarkable difference in attitude in comparison to every other generation, but they weren't born out of something positive either. Their name, Baby Boomers, comes from the fact that in the era they were born, couples and parents rushed to have them—parents rushed to have babies before the soldiers were called for war. This caused a massive increase in birthrates, resulting in a generation we know as Boomers. This is the complete opposite of the low birth rates that happened during the Silent Generation.

However, the birthrate wasn't the only thing that was picked up in America. Parents now have access to successful birth control, which means that if a baby was born, it wasn't born out of an accident. But because of the war, most parents during this era were extremely focused on family—they wanted families, and they wanted bigger, thought-out families. And families they have.

But what did the Baby Boomers signify? What did they fight for? The Baby Boomers came into their prime age around the '60s and '70s, a time of Civil Rights Movements and protests against wars like the Vietnam War. They were, and still are, a generation that shaped the way America is today.

Gen X

Not to be confused with Gen Z, Gen X is the generation that was born between 1965 and 1980 (*Gen X*, 2021). If you wanted to sum up a generation in one song, then the song you would listen to is a song called *Video Killed the Radio Star* by *The Buggles*. This is because this generation is known for one thing: MTV.

This generation is like no other. They experienced things for the first time like no other generation had seen. They saw a rise in the music industry, seeing genres like hip-hop, punk rock, and grunge rise to fame on the channel where they all lived and breathed. This generation saw plenty of other things, though. Things like the rise in computers and cellphones and the development of amazing products and businesses like Apple and IBM have.

But this generation wasn't scared. They fought like no other generation could. On the scene of 9/11, you saw Gen X fight through the rubble to save souls. They were there at the forefront, fighting some of the most horrific occurrences any generation has ever seen.

But this generation wasn't only known for its fighting spirit and the growing music scene. They were prominent in the entrepreneurial world too, coming up with brand-new ideas and products no one else could have ever thought of. This is the generation responsible for Apple, Amazon, Google, and YouTube. All the applications and products we know and love today. Gen X walked so Gen Z could run.

Millennials

We've mentioned Millennials briefly at the beginning of this book, where we chatted a bit more about who and what they are. Let's refresh our memories with a little bit more detail about the generation we know as Millennials.

A Millennial is anyone born between the years 1981 and 1996 (Zelazko, 2023). But where did they come up with the name *Millennial*? These kids—who aren't kids anymore—received their names from Neil Howe and William Strause because they were going to reach adulthood in the new millennium—the 2000s. But other than a distinct name, what makes this generation so edgy and different from any other generation?

Well, millennials are a much larger generation than even the Baby Boomers—they are the biggest generation to walk this planet thus far. And the thing that made them different was not the fact that they grew up in strenuous times—they didn't. As a generation, they grew up in the most stable economic America during a time when America was great again. As a matter of fact, they don't know America is in a state of peril, whereas, as a country, they only got richer and richer.

But despite this stability and sunshine, there were plenty of dark days. One of the darkest days every Millennial will remember is 9/11—an event that would eventually define their adulthood. This generation saw war, too, during Iraq and Afghanistan, and almost as if their adulthood was doomed, they saw the Great Recession of 2007–2009.

But what does this mean for Millennials? Well, it meant that these great kids could not achieve the achievements of their parents and grandparents, and plenty of them still struggle with commodities like buying a house and paying for rent.

Even during these strenuous times, Millennials saw the rise of something amazing, something lifechanging. They saw the rise of the Internet. Around the time these kids just came into adulthood or late teenhood, they were introduced to something we know as the Internet. They saw a rise in the use of smartphones, laptops, and TVs. Out of all the generations, they were the most eager to jump on the social media and streaming bandwagon.

They started to use social media the way we would see Gen Z use it—to communicate with their friends, keep up with families, and even date. Millennials contributed to these applications just as much as they enjoyed using them, birthing the father of social media, Mark Zuckerberg.

Generational Conflict

We all know people from different generations butt heads at times—it's not really a secret. It's probably a boat we find ourselves in more often than we'd like. But we fight and argue, not because we want to, but because we believe in something and we are fighting for the cause. This is what makes generational conflict so tricky—every generation has different beliefs and different values, and when values don't match up, conflict ensues.

Common examples of generational conflict are when a younger employee or family member feels like they don't have enough responsibility or when an older person can't understand the use of technology. To top this off, there are often personality clashes too, which makes the existing conflict even more fiery than it already is.

The only thing we can do is understand the importance of resolving the conflict and identify it far before it even starts. Let's chat about some common sources of generational conflict and how to resolve them.

Common Sources of Conflict

Values and Priorities

What we often forget is that the way we are brought up influences our values and priorities in life greatly. The environment we are raised in and the type of childhood we have to influence the way we see the world and change the way we need things. This can also influence the values in our lives and the things we prioritize. Most of all, our childhoods influence who we become as adults. Think about it—a person who lacked a childhood completely, a person who had to grow up very quickly, has far different priorities and values than a person who was allowed to nurture their childhood.

So, which generation values what, and how can it cause conflict?

Well, Baby Boomers value their work. We might as well call them the workaholic generation. They value a competitive spirit, but that's not because a little bit of competition is always good—they value a competitive spirit because when they were younger, the boom in marriages and the births of children caused resources to be spread thin across a nation. This forced the typical Boomer perspective: Work hard for what you need—and then work even harder next time. But there are plenty of good values that Boomers are more than welcome to share with the world—like the fact that they are goal-oriented, career-focused, and self-actualized. This combination is amazing when it comes to flourishing in your career, but not the friendliest of combinations for a family life.

You can imagine the fights their workaholic natures caused in their family lives—the biggest conflict in a Baby Boomer's life.

Gen X saw the mistakes that the Baby Boomers made and tried everything in their power not to be like the Boomers. With Gen X, you find that they value a good work-life balance. They wholeheartedly discarded a workaholic lifestyle, valuing time with their family and their hobbies instead.

Gen X is a generation that values its independence. As a generation, they had to adapt to a quick and sudden change—everything in their lives went from being analog to digital—tapes, video cameras, everything. This means that, as a generation, they had to adapt quickly. This also made them exceptionally malleable in a work environment where they adapted the saying, *work hard, play hard.* As a generation, they are also more materialistic. They obtained these values because they were raised after a war, saw what war did to their parents and grandparents, and tried to avoid anything to become like them.

As you can imagine, being materialistic and independent has caused many fights for Gen X, some of them because they no longer communicate with family, others because they spend money on things because they want it, not necessarily because they can afford it.

Millennials, on the other hand, are the first generation affected by the digital takeover. This generation had to adapt even faster than Gen X did before them because if they didn't adapt, they would have been left for dead. But alongside the digital takeover came the fact that there was a sudden boom in communication. Instead of being a stubborn generation like the generations before them, Millennials absorbed as much as they could from the generations before them.

They learned from 9/11, ensuring something as catastrophic would not happen again, and they valued the fact that Gen X prioritized work-life balance.

With this extremely volatile environment, Millennials decided to become the most malleable generation yet. They value work, but they only value a work environment that aligns with their needs. They value communication and hard work, but they will not value anything that breaks their flexibility or breaks down their personal development journey. They want to learn, they want to grow, and they want to work, but they also want to play.

This leaves us with Gen Z... the first global generation (Odukoya, 2022). This generation is like no other, and they are doing everything in their power to be different from the other generations.

How Gen Z Differs from Each Generation & How to Overcome It

Respect Differences

Gen Z is going to be different for you. They are not going to change for you. They are not going to be more like you if you express that your values do not align, and they are definitely not going to adapt to your values. The easiest thing you can do is accept the fact that you have differences.

Chances are, Gen Z already respects your opinion and your values—remember, as a generation, they value diversity, and diversity doesn't just mean skin color or culture. It means opinion and perspective, too. Remember, Gen Z has different priorities and different values because they are at different stages in their lives. Gen Z values technological integration, social and environmental issues, diversity and inclusion, work-life balance, innovation, financial stability, and authenticity. Once you know what they value and why they value it, you can realize that perhaps some of those values and responsibilities even align with some of yours.

Empathize

This might be the most challenging way to resolve conflict with a Gen Zer. By trying to put yourself in their shoes at their age, you can understand what they are going through much easier. You can try to imagine how they feel and what they must be going through, and this act will give you a much better idea of where they are in their lives. Remember, the conflict between generations comes from the fact that different people are at different stages of their lives and were raised in different ways. If you can understand where someone came from, you can easily understand why they act the way they do.

Be Honest

We know Gen Z values honesty and transparency, so why not try to use it when you want to resolve conflict? Tell Gen Z exactly what bothers you and what you think they're doing wrong—be open and clear. The key is not to be aggressive or to make them feel like they are being attacked. The key to good communication is to do it calmly and to think it through.

Once you can figure out what the underlying cause of the issue is, like perhaps you are struggling with something technological or there is a core value that doesn't align, you can discuss the way forward and seal up the open, gaping wound that is the conflict between generations. The key to conflict resolution is open and clear communication where both parties feel safe and secure enough to let their emotions and thoughts out freely.

Compromise

Difficult differences and conflicts aren't always slap-on-a-band-aid-and-call-it-a-day situations. Sometimes, it can leave heaps of scars and damage to relationships. But before it gets there, consider compromising, even if you don't want to. A compromise is always better than leaving a situation to get worse.

Try to work with the Gen Zer you are experiencing conflict with—try to have a calm and relaxed conversation to find a middle ground.

Chapter 10: Supporting Gen Z's Goals & Aspirations

What is your wildest dream? Is it possible to own your own little coffee shop in the corner of your town? Was it to be in a world-renowned rock band? Or was your biggest desire in life to own your own business?

Whatever it was, it was a dream. It was something you could set goals to achieve. It was something you could work hard for. We all have dreams. We all have ambitions, goals, and desires we would love to accomplish in our lives. Sometimes, we want to try to achieve these goals by ourselves, but most of the time, we realize that a little help can go a very long way.

We are all here to help each other. As humans, we love to help. We love to be involved. We want to be involved. And it's not like we are being involved because we have to—we love feeling useful. We love feeling appreciated. We love doing things for other people, especially when they can't do things for themselves.

Gen Z is no different. They are a generation filled with hopes and dreams, much like every generation was at the young age they are. They want to make big things happen, and they want to live meaningful lives. The least we can do is try to help Gen Z along their journey and make their journey memorable, lovable, and, most of all, easier than our journey ever was.

Gen Z's Goals

Gen Z's goals and aspirations might look a little bit different than our goals and aspirations, but that is for no other reason than the fact that they are younger than we are. They might be only a few years younger if you are a millennial, or they might be decades younger if you are older. You can't expect a kid and an adult to have the same hopes and dreams, so before you start your journey to support Gen Z, realize that their dreams are going to look different, and that's okay. It's okay for their dreams to be ambitious, odd, and crazy.

So let's dive in.

A Great Career

If you had to ask a Gen Z kid what they prefer: A good salary or a good career, they are most likely to answer neither. They want a job that aligns with their values. Of course, having a fulfilling job comes in second, but the most important thing for a Gen Z kid is to find a career worth pursuing that aligns with what they believe in. To them, salary is just a number, because they are willing to take a job if it allows them to learn.

In the second place, they want a job that allows them a flexible schedule where they can work when it suits them best. These kids value their mental health, and they value their jobs, so to make sure that they deliver the best quality work, they want to be able to deliver it on their terms. This is why you'll see that most of the new Gen Z kids on the block want to work from home instead of coming into the office.

They want a fulfilling, happy career where they can learn and work on their own terms—but money would definitely be a bonus!

Homes

Believe it or not, this generation wants nothing to do with kids. Starting a family? Nope? School fees? Not a chance. But buying a home? Count them in, as in yesterday.

Most of the Gen Z adults, or quite a large amount of the Gen Z population at the moment, say that owning a house is far more important to them than starting a family or even stepping into marriage. As a matter of fact, on their list of priorities, marriage comes in last, and having kids comes in second. Their first priority will always be to own a home (Commisso, 2023).

When it comes to owning a home, millennials would tell you that things are not looking great at the moment. However, certain Gen Z adults hit the COVID-19 pandemic at the right age—when they were financially stable and when interest rates dropped. This allows them to own a home between eighteen and twenty-four. Can you imagine owning a home at that age? Because Millennials definitely can't. They remember fondly how difficult it was to become financially stable at that age and remember wanting a home but being unable to afford one.

International Life

Gen Z has absolutely no desire to stay in their home country. They want to hit the road—and they want to hit it sooner rather than later. A whopping 55% of Gen Z adults see themselves moving abroad to a different country (Commisso, 2023). These kids don't want to be stuck with the same old life they've seen for the past few years—they are ready for something new and fresh. If we know anything about Gen Z, we know that they would definitely value the inclusivity and diversity of experiencing life abroad, so perhaps it's not that bad of an idea!

Side Hustles

Gen Z is not afraid to work—and yes, Karen, they might not want to work for your company, but they sure as hell will work for themselves. 52% of Gen Z kids want to work for themselves—they don't want to be bossed around by someone else, and they definitely don't want to make money for someone else (*The Ambitions of Gen Z: Balancing Happiness, Work, and Financial Goals*, 2024). That means that one in five Gen Zers wants to own and operate their own businesses or become a self-employed contractor.

Supporting Gen Z in Achieving Their Goals

In this book, we've already discussed a few strategies for how you can help Gen Z become a better person. Some of those strategies include becoming their mentor and guiding them through life, while other methods are less practical, like just lending them an ear and listening to them.

But there are many ways you can help a Gen Zer reach their goals without being a mentor to them.

You can start off by helping Gen Z establish what goals they have. This can be done by asking them the straight question—what are your goals? What do you want from life? Why do you want it? By asking these important questions, you are delving into the depths of their brains and figuring out what makes them tick and what their goals are. Chat with them about how their goals align with their values and their beliefs—by getting all the information you can out of them, you are getting a better understanding of these goals and ambitions.

If you have all the information you need, you can help Gen Zer create a strategy to turn these goals into a reality. A strategy is the most difficult part of having dreams and ambitions, and this is usually the part where we all need a little bit of help and encouragement. When it comes to strategy, most people realize that their dreams are way too big for them to achieve and give up—but the strategy is only the beginning. You can only climb a mountain if you start with the first step.

Sometimes, it's difficult to start a strategy from scratch, especially when you have no idea where to begin, so begin by asking Gen Zer what exactly they want to do. By now, they must have an idea of how they want to reach their goals. If they want to buy a house, then they know they must first save up for the downpayment. If they want to move abroad, they need money for work visas, and they need to find a job. If they can define what they need, you can help them strategize exactly what their first steps are going to be to make their dreams come true.

After establishing the first few steps of the strategy, it is easier to bunch together the second and third bite-sized goals to climb the mountain at a slow and steady pace.

Once you have a plan together, you can establish what the obstacles will be. It's important to identify obstacles because obstacles are the first reason people quit their dreams and aspirations. If you can identify the obstacles, you can create an action plan to overcome them. In turn, your goals and ambitions will remain right on track.

Perhaps Gen Zers will cross paths with obstacles on their way to achieving their goals—if that happens, it's your job to motivate them not to quit. It's your responsibility as a good civilian to help them, and to be honest, you'll probably enjoy encouraging them too. But they haven't started following their goals yet, so let's not jump the gun.

The first step to any goal is to begin. When you tackle the goals with your Gen Z mentee, make sure that you encourage them to follow the action plan. The plan is there for a reason—to help them achieve their goal. There is no point in putting all this effort into a goal-achieving plan if they are not going to use it. The beauty of this plan is that you can easily adjust it as you go along the journey, so if something doesn't work, just change it.

Once the plan is in motion and they're finally working towards their goals, don't forget about them. Check in with them, make sure they are still on track, and ask them how it is going. This regular check-in will do wonders to encourage them to stay on the right road and not go off the beaten track. When the time comes, you can celebrate their small wins with them and, eventually, the big wins. But never, ever forget about the small victories; sometimes, they are just as important as the big ones.

And hopefully, by the time they reach their goal, you can proudly announce that you were part of their success.

Conclusion

And there you have it, folks! You've now unlocked the secret codes to understand and connect with the elusive species known as Gen Z. From decoding their emoji-filled messages to deciphering their TikTok dances; you're now equipped to navigate the digital wilderness they call home.

Remember, fellow Millennials, it's not about trying to be "hip" or "cool" (if those words are even still in their vocabulary). It's about genuine understanding and respect for the generation shaping our future. So, whether you're a seasoned Baby Boomer trying to figure out Snapchat filters or a Gen Xer attempting to decode Gen Z slang, fear not! With a sprinkle of empathy, a dash of patience, and a generous helping of memes, you too can bridge the intergenerational gap.

So go forth, my friends, armed with your newfound knowledge and a willingness to embrace the unknown. Whether it's discussing the latest meme trends or championing social causes, let's join hands (virtually, of course) and embark on this journey together. After all, the key to Gen Z is not just understanding them but also celebrating their unique perspectives and contributions to our ever-evolving world.

And who knows? Maybe, just maybe, with a little bit of effort and a whole lot of laughter, we'll find ourselves not just connecting with Gen Z but becoming honorary members of their squad. Now, if you'll excuse me, I've got some TikTok tutorials to catch up on. Peace out, fam!

Glossary

Authenticity: Authenticity is the act of being authentic. When you are authentic, it means that you are not a copy of something or someone else—you are unique and yourself.

Boomers/Baby Boomers: Any person born between 1949 and 1964.

Big Yikes: A phrase used to express disapproval, shock, or embarrassment.

Digital Landscape: A collection of digital assets that a specific target audience uses to get information from, i.e., a website, smartphone, videos, or social media.

Digital Native: A person who was raised in an age where digital technology was easily accessible. They had exposure to technology from a young age.

Diversity: Differences in humans, like race, ethnicity, gender, identity, age, social class, sexual orientation, and the act of including all of these people.

Fairycore: A fashion theme inspired by fantasy and fairies.

Fam: Family.

Gen Alpha: Any person born between 2010 and 2024.

Gen X: Any person born between 1965 and 1980.

Gen Z: Any person born between 1997 and 2012.

Generational Differences: The difference in behavior, values, and communication styles between different generations could cause friction.

Global Awareness: Gaining knowledge on a global scale about intercultural issues, trends, and systems.

Gram: Instagram.

Helicopter Parent: An overprotective parent.

Instagram: An app created to allow people to share photos with their peers and loved ones who follow them.

Meme: A humorous piece of media, usually text, video, or image, shared across the internet between internet users.

Millennial: Any person born between 1981 and 1996.

No cap: No lie/for real.

Reels: Short videos, usually under 1 minute, recorded in 1080px x 1920px and shared on Instagram by Facebook.

Reddit: A social media app where people can share their thoughts, news, questions, and advice.

Rizz: Short for charisma.

Self Care: The act of taking time to look after your mental health through calming activities.

Side Hustle: Extra work outside the primary source of income to make extra money. A way to earn an extra income through a unique skill or business spirit.

Silent Generation: Any person born between 1928 and 1946.

Social Injustice: A group of people being treated differently because they are not conforming to societal norms. People who have a disadvantage based on cultural or ethnic differences.

Social Media: A place online where people can share information and ideas.

Stan: A combination of the words "stalker" and "fan." When you stan something or someone, it means that you support them.

Sus: Short for Suspicious.

TikTok: A video-sharing application.

References

Authenticity is key: Reaching the Gen Z consumer. (n.d.). EMARKETER. Retrieved March 20, 2024, from https://www.emarketer.com/content/authenticity-key-reaching-gen-z-consumer-sponsored-content

Benveniste, A. (2022, January 26). *The Meaning and History of Memes.* The New York Times. https://www.nytimes.com/2022/01/26/crosswords/what-is-a-meme.html

Brave. (2023, October 13). *How Gen Z Are Using Social Media Differently.* Brave Agency. https://www.brave.agency/how-gen-z-are-using-social-media-differently/

Capoot, A., Piazza, J., & Khan, M. (2023, October 17). *How Gen Z uses technology — flip phones, digital cameras, voice memos.* CNBC. https://www.cnbc.com/2023/10/17/how-genz-uses-tech-flip-phones-digital-cameras-voice-memos.html

Carnegie, M. (2022, August 8). *Gen Z: How Young People Are Changing Activism.* BBC.com. https://www.bbc.com/worklife/article/20220803-gen-z-how-young-people-are-changing-activism

Clark, C. (2022, June 27). *Generation Y And Z - Empowered Or Entitled?* Forbes. https://www.forbes.com/sites/charlestowersclark/2022/06/27/generation-y-and-zempowered-or-entitled/

Communication Style: A Full Guide About the "Instant" Gen. (n.d.). Deskbird. https://www.deskbird.com/blog/generation-z-communication-preferences

De Witte, M. (2022, January 3). *What to Know about Gen Z.* Stanford News. https://news.stanford.edu/2022/01/03/know-gen-z/

Dimock, M. (2019, January 17). *Defining generations: Where Millennials end and Generation Z begins.* Pew Research Center. https://www.pewresearch.org/short-reads/2019/01/17/where-millennials-end-and-generation-z-begins/

Earls, A. (2017, September 29). *10 Traits of Generation Z.* Lifeway Research. https://research.lifeway.com/2017/09/29/10-traits-of-generation-z/?cmpid=pm:ggl:220914

Gen X. (2021, April 23). Visual Capitalist. https://www.visualcapitalist.com/gpi/gen-x/Gen Z

Gen Z Demands Diversity and Inclusion in the Workplace. (n.d.). World Economic Forum. https://www.weforum.org/videos/1-in-2-gen-z-ers-won-t-work-in-a-place-without-diverse-leadership/

Generation Z And Their Phones: Separating The Myths From The Facts. (2020, September 22). Shout out UK. https://www.shoutoutuk.org/2020/09/22/generation-z-and-their-phones-separating-the-myths-from-the-facts/

Hofstra Marketing and Communications. (2021, March 26). *How Technology Addiction Is Impacting Generation Z.* News |

Hofstra University, New York. https://news.hofstra.edu/2021/03/26/how-technology-addiction-is-impacting-generation-z/

How Do We Cope With Generational Conflict? (n.d.). The Wellness Corner. https://www.thewellnesscorner.com/blog/generational-conflict

How Gen Z Is Changing Social Media. (n.d.). LinkedIn. https://www.linkedin.com/pulse/how-gen-z-changing-social-media-hgs-interactive/

How Gen Z is Shaping the Future of Technology. (2023, May 5). Amber Student. https://amberstudent.com/blog/post/how-gen-z-is-shaping-the-future-of-technology

How the interests of Gen Z are different from other generations. (2023, April 5). Voxpopme. https://www.voxpopme.com/market-research-blog/understanding-gen-z/

How to Win Gen Z's Trust? (n.d.). 20Something. Retrieved April 13, 2024, from https://20something.be/2023/09/14/how-to-win-gen-zs-trust/

Hughes, J. (2022, August 24). *Communicating with Generation Z: Everything You Need to Know.* Keg. https://www.keg.com/news/communicating-with-generation-z-everything-you-need-to-know

Hughes, Z. (2023, August 28). *Help Others Achieve Their Goals.* LinkedIn. https://www.linkedin.com/pulse/help-others-achieve-goals-zach-hughes/

Impact 360. (2022, January 27). *Gen Z: The Most Anxious Generation.* Impact 360 Institute. https://www.impact360institute.org/articles/anxiety-and-empowerment-in-gen

Indeed. (2022). *Benefits of Diversity in the Workplace: Five to Consider.* Indeed. https://www.indeed.com/hire/c/info/benefits-of-diversity

Irvine, M. (2023, August 1). *What Is the Biggest Misconception of Gen Z in the Workplace?* LinkedIn. https://www.linkedin.com/business/talent/blog/learning-and-development/what-is-biggest-misconception-of-gen-z-in-workplace

Kearns, M. (2023, September 14). *Gen Z's Trust Issues.* National Review. https://www.nationalreview.com/corner/gen-zs-trust-issues/

Ken, C. (n.d.). *Understanding Generational Differences* [PDF]. KELD. Retrieved March 25, 2024, from https://www2.ca.uky.edu/agcomm/pubs/cld1/cld18/cld18.PDF

Khan, A. (2023, December 8). *The most diverse generation in the workplace can agree on this one career-builder.* Fast Company. https://www.fastcompany.com/90993038/gen-z-career-builder-mentoring

Lange, C. (2023, April 8). *The Importance of Diversity and Inclusivity in Marketing to Gen Z*. Medium. https://medium.com/@charleslangeconsultant/the-importance-of-diversity-and-inclusivity-in-marketing-to-gen-z-6c8597aa7ab1

Leadership, T. I. of. (2022). *How mentoring benefits Gen Z and beyond.* Leadership.global. https://leadership.global/resourceLibrary/helping-them-rise-how-mentoring-benefits-gen-z-and-beyond.html#:~:text=Benefits%20of%20mentoring

Mason, M. C., Zamparo, G., Marini, A., & Ameen, N. (2022). Glued to your phone? Generation Z's smartphone addiction and online compulsive buying. *Computers in Human Behavior, 136*, 107404. https://doi.org/10.1016/j.chb.2022.107404

McKinsey. (2022). *What is diversity, equity, and inclusion (DE&I)?* McKinsey & Company. https://www.mckinsey.com/featured-insights/mckinsey-explainers/what-is-diversity-equity-and-inclusion

Merriman, M. (n.d.). *How can understanding the influence of Gen Z today empower your tomorrow?* EY. https://www.ey.com/en_us/consulting/generational-dynamics/2023-gen-z-study

Millennials vs Gen Z: Key Differences. (n.d.). Adecco. https://www.adecco.com/en-us/employers/resources/article/generation-z-vs-millennials-infographic

Mind Tools Content Team. (2023). *MindTools | Home*. Mind Tools. https://www.mindtools.com/ay3oirc/authenticity

Montagner, Q. (2023, December 28). *How to Build Trust with Gen Z*. Koya Digital. https://koyadigital.co/how-to-build-trust-with-gen-z/

Nwanonyiri, C. (2023, June 17). *Exploring The Pros And Cons In Gen Z's Digital Journey*. Tech Build Africa. https://techbuild.africa/exploring-pros-and-cons-gen-z-digital-journey/

Odukoya, A. (2022, November 17). *The Changing Generational Values*. Johns Hopkins University. https://imagine.jhu.edu/blog/2022/11/17/the-changing-generational-values/

Out Of The Box. (2016, June 6). *How Do You Support Someone In Achieving Their Dreams?* Coaching out of the Box®. https://coachingoutofthebox.com/coaching-resources/blog/how-do-you-support-someone-in-achieving-their-dreams-2/

Overlund, M. A. (2020, April 13). *Trust, Integrity, and Authenticity*. Leadership & Vision. https://medium.com/leadership-vision/trust-integrity-and-authenticity-9aff8e6c2abb

Parker, K., & Igielnik, R. (2020, May 14). *On the Cusp of Adulthood and Facing an Uncertain Future: What We Know about Gen Z so Far*. Pew Research Center. https://www.pewresearch.org/social-trends/2020/05/14/on-the-cusp-of-adulthood-and-facing-an-uncertain-future-what-we-know-about-gen-z-so-far-2/

Pew Research Center. (2008, June 25). *Baby Boomers: The Gloomiest Generation.* Pew Research Center's Social & Demographic Trends Project. https://www.pewresearch.org/social-trends/2008/06/25/baby-boomers-the-gloomiest-generation/

Rodriguez, A. (2022, July 14). *Gen-Z: The Most Diverse Generation in the Workplace.* Insight Global. https://insightglobal.com/blog/gen-z-diversity-in-the-workplace/

Servaes, S., Choudhury, P., & Parikh, A. K. (2022). What is diversity? *Pediatric Radiology, 52*(9). Springer. https://doi.org/10.1007/s00247-022-05356-0

Shinaver, D. (2024, March 22). *Nurturing the Next Generation: Strategies for Fostering Growth and Loyalty Among Young Talent.* LinkedIn. https://www.linkedin.com/pulse/nurturing-next-generation-strategies-fostering-growth-daniel-shinaver-07x6c/

Shriber, S. (2023, June 14). *Gen Z's Future Goals – Top Insights on Careers, Homeownership and More.* CivicScience. https://civicscience.com/gen-zs-future-goals-top-insights-on-careers-homeownership-and-more/

Shufeldt, J. (2022, September 17). *The Hardest Aspects About Being an Entrepreneur.* LinkedIn. https://www.linkedin.com/pulse/hardest-aspects-being-entrepreneur-john-shufeldt-md-jd-mba-facep/

Smith, R. (2020, December 2). *Why is the Silent Generation Called "Silent"?* FamilySearch Blog. https://www.familysearch.org/en/blog/silent-generation-characteristics

Sushantvohra. (2023, September 10). *Gen Z is Rewriting Rules About Entrepreneurship.* Medium. https://medium.com/@sushantvohra/gen-z-is-rewriting-rules-about-entrepreneurship-da80de5f63d0

The Ambitions of Gen Z: Balancing Happiness, Work, and Financial Goals. (2024, February 6). EduBirdie. https://edubirdie.com/blog/life-goals-of-gen-z

The Baby Boom. (n.d.). Khan Academy. https://www.khanacademy.org/humanities/us-history/postwarera/postwar-era/a/the-baby-boom

Thornbury, C. (n.d.). *Active Listening: A Guide to Building Trust with your Team.* Leave Dates. Retrieved April 13, 2024, from https://www.leavedates.com/articles/active-listening-skills#:~:text=Listening%20and%20acting%20builds%20trust&text=One%20way%20to%20build%20trustTowers-

Trecartin, C. (2023, March 2). *Why does Gen Z Crave Authenticity Over Everything Else?* Medium. https://medium.com/@chartrecar/why-does-gen-z-crave-authenticity-over-everything-else-6143b2653dd7

Vasey, G. (2023, August 11). *Gen Z consumers seek authentic brands they can trust.* CX Today. https://www.cxtoday.com/voice-of-the-customer/gen-z-consumers-seek-authentic-brands-they-can-

trust/#:~:text=Authenticity%20is%20the%20new%20curre
ncy

What are Millennials? (n.d.). Bamboohr.
https://www.bamboohr.com/resources/hr-
glossary/millennials

What is digital storytelling? | Digital Storytelling. (n.d.).
Blogs.brighton.
https://blogs.brighton.ac.uk/digitalstorytelling/what-is-
digital-storytelling/

What is gen Z? (2023, March 20). Mckinsey & Company.
https://www.mckinsey.com/featured-insights/mckinsey-
explainers/what-is-gen-z

What workforce diversity means for Gen Z. (n.d.). Monster.
https://hiring.monster.com/resources/workforce-
management/diversity-in-the-workplace/workforce-
diversity-for-millennials/

Youth's watching habits: How is Gen Z consuming video? (2023,
May 23). BroadPeak. https://broadpeak.tv/blog/what-gen-z-
watch/

Zelazko, A. (2023, June 29). *Millennials | demographic group |
Britannica.* Britannica.
https://www.britannica.com/topic/millennial

Zimmer, S. (n.d.). *Building Trust with Millennials and Gen Z.*
Bridgeworks.
https://www.generations.com/insights/building-trust-with-
millennials-and-gen-z